AMAZING
NIGHT SKY
ATLAS

Project managed by: Tall Tree Ltd
Author: Nancy Dickmann
Consultant: David Hawksett
Illustrator: Andrew Painter (Beehive Illustration)
Designer: Ben Ruocco
Editors: Rob Colson, Nicola Hodgson
Publisher: Piers Pickard
Editorial Director: Joe Fullman
Art Director: Andy Mansfield
Print Production: Nigel Longuet

Published in August 2022 by Lonely Planet Global Ltd
CRN: 554153

ISBN: 978 1 83869 512 5

Printed in Singapore
10 9 8 7 6 5 4 3 2 1

STAY IN TOUCH:
lonelyplanet.com/contact

Lonely Planet Office:
IRELAND
Digital Depot, Roe Lane (off Thomas St),
Digital Hub, Dublin 8, D08 TCV4

MIX
Paper from
responsible sources
FSC™ C021741

Paper in this book is certified against the
Forest Stewardship Council™ standards.
FSC™ promotes environmentally responsible,
socially beneficial and economically viable
management of the world's forests.

lonely planet KIDS

AMAZING
NIGHT SKY
ATLAS

written by Nancy Dickmann

CONTENTS

INTRODUCTION

The sky is full of wonders. Gaze up on a dark night and you'll see hundreds – maybe even thousands – of twinkling stars. And hidden among their pinpricks of light are a host of other objects: planets, asteroids, comets and even spacecraft! It's all there, if you know where to look.

The billions of stars of the Milky Way form a great cloud in the night sky.

WHAT'S OUT THERE?

As you look up at the sky, you are standing on a small, rocky planet. It's just one of eight planets travelling round our Sun, forming the Solar System. But the Sun is just one of the billions of stars that make up our galaxy, the Milky Way. And the Milky Way is just one of billions of galaxies in the Universe! It's a lot to take in, but this book will help you do it. Read on to discover what's in the sky and how to find it. You'll learn to navigate your way around the stars, using their patterns to hop from one constellation to another. You'll discover how to tell a planet from a star, how to spot a space station, and how to use a telescope. You'll also learn that, despite all we know about the sky, there are still a lot of mysteries to be solved. One day, perhaps you could be the one to solve them! Are you ready to travel to the stars? Your journey begins here.

Drawing constellations helps us to map the night sky.

HISTORY OF THE NIGHT SKY

Look up! The stars may look as though they're randomly sprinkled across the sky, but they each occupy a specific position – although the pattern shifts from one night to the next. Meanwhile, the planets change their position over time. By watching and taking notes, you'll start to see patterns emerge. Humans have tracked these patterns for thousands of years.

The night sky has been a source of wonder for millennia.

This 17th-century map shows the positions of stars with constellations drawn on them for the Northern (left) and Southern (right) Hemispheres.

SHAPES AND STORIES

It's easy to look up and spot arrangements of stars that resemble animals or figures, and it's tempting to make up stories about them. But if you know what the patterns are, and how they work, the night sky becomes a map and a calendar all rolled into one. You can use the stars to find your way, anticipate the changing of the seasons and even predict when the Moon will turn blood-red, or the Sun will disappear in the middle of the day. Writing was invented about 5,500 years ago, and we have no idea how much people before that understood about the movement of the heavens. However, archaeologists have found clues in objects, cave paintings and some of the structures they built. For example, prehistoric peoples built the great circle of stones now known as Stonehenge, in England, about 5,500 years ago. Its standing stones are aligned so that, at the summer solstice, the Sun rises over one of the main stones. At the winter solstice, the setting Sun is framed by some of the tallest stones.

Sunrise at Stonehenge

A blood moon happens during a total lunar eclipse.

ANCIENT PEOPLES AND THE SKY

Early peoples were stargazers, not astronomers. Although they watched the skies, they weren't trying to figure out the science of how it all worked, like modern astronomers do. Instead, to them the stars and planets were something more mystical, or even magical. Their patterns and movements were often woven into a culture's religion.

BABYLONIAN ASTRONOMERS

The Babylonian people, who lived in Mesopotamia 3000 years ago, watched the sky because they believed that any changes were signs from the gods. They could be warning them that war, famine or plague was on the way. And the Babylonians weren't alone in these beliefs! Many cultures around the world believed that the heavens and the world of the gods were linked.

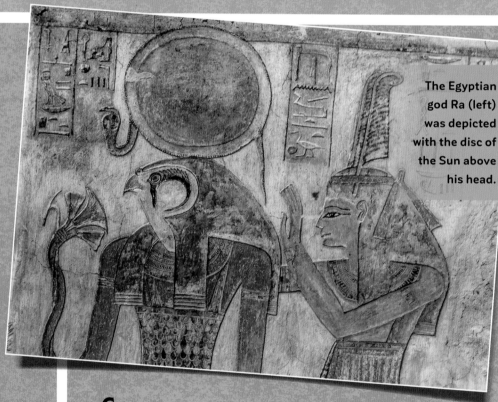

The Egyptian god Ra (left) was depicted with the disc of the Sun above his head.

The ancient Babylonians recorded their observations on clay tablets.

STARS AND GODS

For many peoples, the stars and planets were the embodiments of gods, and the Sun was often the most important. In Egypt, it was worshipped as the god Ra. For others, the stars represented souls. Some of these beliefs still live on today. The Karanga people of South Africa believe that stars are the eyes of the dead, while the neighbouring Tswana people think the stars are the spirits of people yet to be born.

Myths and Legends

Like many other cultures, the ancient Greeks made up stories to explain the constellations that they saw. Some of these stories are more than 3000 years old. For example, the Greeks believed that the god Zeus put the twin brothers Castor and Pollux in the sky as the constellation we now call Gemini. The arrangement of the constellations told stories – for instance, the hunter Orion, pictured left, is surrounded in the sky by constellations representing animals for him to hunt (see pages 116–119). The myths say that he was killed by stepping on a scorpion, so the gods placed the constellation Scorpius on the opposite side of the sky, so that it could never hurt him again.

The Beginning of Astronomy

In Babylon in the 7th century BCE, scribes who worked at the city's temples were sent to read the stars every night, making records on clay tablets. They could then spot patterns in the ways that the Moon and planets moved. Later, Chinese and Greek astronomers applied their knowledge of geometry to the heavens to work out the size and distance of the Sun, Moon and stars, and to map how they move in relation to each other using models called armillary spheres.

A modern armillary sphere

TELLING STORIES

Although many people around the world look up at the same skies, they see them a bit differently. Throughout the centuries, different cultures have come up with their own interpretations of the night sky. They have told stories and created myths about the shapes that they see.

People still love to tell stories about the stars.

The pattern of stars known as the Plough or the Big Dipper

IT'S ALL GREEK TO ME

Many of the constellations used in the Western world come from the ancient Greeks. They believed in a world filled with gods, goddesses, heroes and magical creatures, and many of these characters are found in the stars. The Greeks often took constellations that had been picked out by earlier civilisations and updated them to reflect their own heroes and villains.

LADLE OR CARIBOU?

The Plough (see page 97) is a good example of people interpreting stars in different ways. With its seven stars forming a boxy shape with a handle, it's one of the most recognisable patterns in the night sky. To astronomers, this is part of a larger constellation called Ursa Major, or the Great Bear (see pages 108–109). To people in the UK, it's the Plough. To Americans, who see it as a ladle shape, it's the Big Dipper. To the Inuit, it's a caribou, and to the Sami people of northern Scandinavia, it's a bow and arrow. Ask a Mongolian, and they'll tell you it's seven Buddhas, while to Macedonians, it's a group of organised thieves!

Perseus and Andromeda

Greek myths tell of King Cepheus and his wife, Cassiopeia, who had a daughter, Andromeda. Cassiopeia liked to boast that her daughter was the most beautiful girl who had ever lived. But her vanity angered the gods. The sea god, Poseidon, let loose a sea beast that began to terrorise Cepheus' kingdom. A priest told Cepheus that the only way to stop it was to sacrifice Andromeda to the beast. So Cepheus and Cassiopeia chained their daughter to a rock and left her to her fate. Luckily, a young man called Perseus happened to be riding by on his flying horse, Pegasus. Perseus was the son of Zeus, the king of the gods, and he was struck by Andromeda's beauty. He made a deal that if he could slay the monster, he could marry Andromeda. And he did! Andromeda was saved, and the characters live on in the constellations Perseus, Pegasus, Andromeda, Cepheus, Cassiopeia and Cetus the sea monster (see pages 114–127).

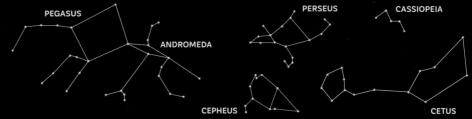

The Lady in the Moon

In China, there is an ancient myth about a beautiful young goddess called Chang'e. As a punishment for breaking some precious porcelain, she was banished from heaven to live on Earth as a mortal. There, she married the famous archer Hou Yi. As thanks for his heroic deeds, Hou Yi had been given a potion that would grant him immortality. But Chang'e missed being a goddess, and she took the elixir and drank it. She floated out of the window and ended up on the Moon, where a white rabbit keeps her company to this day. People say that they can see her in the shadows created by the Moon's craters.

The immortal Chang'e

Some Aboriginal peoples of Australia call this dark patch the Emu.

ᘰARKING THE YEAR

Some stories use the stars as a way of marking the passage of the seasons. In Southern Africa, the Pleiades are known as the 'digging stars' because when they appear in the sky, it's time to start preparing the fields for planting. According to the Namaqua people, the Pleiades (known as *IsiLimela* in their language) were the daughters of the sky god. Their husband shot an arrow at three zebras – the three stars that make up Orion's belt (see page 116). Another version explains the belt by telling of a young girl with magical powers who stared so hard at a group of lions that they turned into stars.

The Pleiades star cluster

ABORIGINAL BELIEFS

Some Aboriginal peoples of Australia see the constellation of Orion (see page 116) as the figure of a man. But in their version, he is the creator god, Baiame. As the constellation sets, he trips and falls over the horizon, making him appear upside-down. The Aboriginal peoples also see patterns in the dark spaces between the stars – as seen in the sweep of the Milky Way. There is one dark patch that they identify as an emu, while the Tupi people of Bolivia and Brazil see it as a different kind of bird called a rhea, which lives in South America.

The god Tezcatlipoca

CREATING THE STARS

The Aztec people, who built a powerful empire in Mexico in the 1400s CE, believed that the stars were there because of the god Tezcatlipoca. He created 400 men and placed them in the skies to be his guardians. The Aztecs also grouped stars into constellations. There was one known as the Scorpion, and another called the Ballcourt, which represented the place where a popular sport was played. It is the same group that forms the Western version of the constellation Gemini (see pages 98–99).

Tiger

The ancient Chinese used animals to represent the sky.

Tortoise

Dragon

Phoenix

ANIMALS IN THE SKY

Chinese astronomers have watched the skies carefully for thousands of years. Like the Babylonians, these ancient stargazers believed that movements in the sky were omens of things that would happen on Earth. They divided the sky into four sections – one for each direction of the compass – surrounding a central area where stars representing the emperor could be found. Each direction represented a season and was symbolised by an animal. North, which was winter, was seen as a black tortoise. A blue dragon represented east and the spring. A red phoenix ruled summer and the southern skies, and a white tiger represented the west and autumn.

NAVIGATING BY THE STARS

Stars are more than just celestial illustrations to the stories we tell – they have a practical use, too. For thousands of years, travellers have used them to find their way. Ancient sailors in the Mediterranean tended to stick close to shore, in sight of landmarks. But other cultures, such as the Polynesians, wanted to go further. They often sailed out of sight of land, and to do that, they needed the stars.

NAVIGATING BY DAY

Imagine you're in a Polynesian outrigger canoe, exploring the islands of the South Pacific. About 4000 years ago, these people began exploring the seas around eastern Asia. They spread eastwards across the Pacific Ocean, 'hopping' from one island to the next in their canoes. They had no maps or compasses, but they had the Sun and stars to navigate by.

Similarly, the Viking people from Scandinavia used the Sun to find their way across Europe and beyond. Vikings used a special 'sunstone' to find the exact location of the Sun, even on a cloudy day. It works by polarising the Sun's light.

SUNSTONE
The Vikings used transparent crystals like this to navigate.

USING THE STARS

At night, the stars take over for navigation. In the Northern Hemisphere, if you can find Polaris (see page 35), that's a start. It always points due north. In the Southern Hemisphere, you can find south by looking for Sigma Octantis. But recognising constellations can help even more. You'll need to know, though, which constellations appear at any particular time of year, and when they rise and set. It's a lot to remember! Because the Polynesians didn't have a written language, navigators would pass their knowledge on from one generation to the next, often in the form of a song.

FINDING LATITUDE

Different cultures eventually invented tools to help use the stars to find their way. The astrolabe was invented in ancient times, though no one knows exactly where or when. It is a tool that helps a sailor measure the angle of a star above the horizon. This is a way of finding out your latitude, or how far north or south you are. An astrolabe had rotating dials that showed the positions of constellations throughout the year. The sextant, invented in 1759, does more or less the same thing as an astrolabe, but it contains a mini-telescope that makes its readings much more accurate.

Top: Astrolabes were used to calculate latitude.

Left: Sextants were also used for celestial navigation.

A marine chronometer

FINDING LONGITUDE

In the past, you could not know your longitude (how far west or east you are) unless you had an accurate clock – and those weren't invented until the 1700s! You can work out your longitude if you know what time it is at a point of known longitude (such as the place where you started your journey). However, pendulum clocks couldn't keep accurate time on a rolling ship. In 1762, John Harrison built a clock, known as a marine chronometer, that could do this. Sailors set it to London time and compared that to the local time, determined by the position of the Sun or stars.

UNLOCKING THE HEAVENS

Scientific breakthroughs often come when someone does things just that little bit differently. In about 1608, spectacle makers in the Netherlands invented the telescope. By putting a pair of lenses into a tube, they made a device that could make faraway objects appear closer.

A Dutch telescope in 1624

SEARCHING THE SKIES

Early telescopes were useful to the military for spotting signals and enemy positions. Then along came the Italian scientist Galileo Galilei, who had the innovative idea of taking one of these 'Dutch perspective glasses' and pointing it at the sky. With one bold move, he had invented telescope astronomy.

Not content with the telescopes made by others, Galileo taught himself how to grind lenses and experimented with making his own telescopes. The first telescopes could magnify objects to three times their actual size. Galileo soon had a telescope that could magnify eight times, and then thirty times.

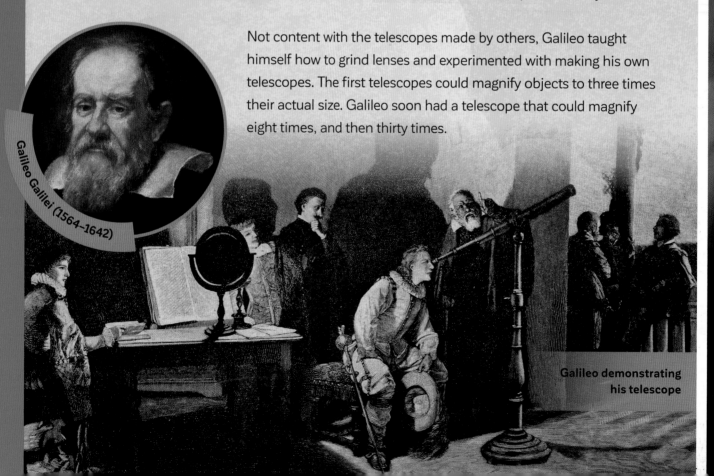

Galileo Galilei (1564–1642)

Galileo demonstrating his telescope

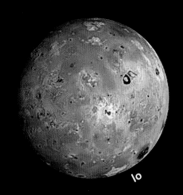

Io

A NEW VIEW

Galileo used his telescope to revolutionise what astronomers knew about the heavens. He spotted mountains and valleys on the surface of the Moon, he researched the phases of Venus, and he found four moons orbiting the planet Jupiter (see pages 68–69).

These discoveries had a huge impact. Most people at the time believed that Earth stayed still while the Sun, Moon, and everything else revolved around it. About 70 years previously, Nicolaus Copernicus (see pages 42–43) had gone against the teachings of the Catholic church by suggesting that, instead, Earth and the planets travel around the Sun. Galileo's observations provided strong evidence that Copernicus had been right.

Europa

Ganymede

Callisto

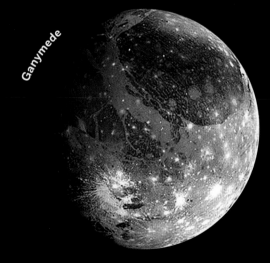

The four largest moons of Jupiter, which were first spotted by Galileo

Full-size reproduction of the Herschel telescope in the Spanish National Observatory

BIGGER AND BETTER

In 1668, the English scientist Isaac Newton invented the reflecting telescope. It replaced one of the lenses with a pair of mirrors, which made it possible to build telescopes that were bigger and more powerful than ever before. Before 1781, people thought there were only six planets, because no one had yet seen beyond Saturn with the naked eye. Then, the British-German astronomer William Herschel (1738–1822) used a 12-metre (40-ft)-long telescope with a mirror 120 centimetres (4 ft) wide to discover the planet Uranus.

WANG ZHENYI

Most astronomers of her time were men, but Wang Zhenyi didn't let that stop her. She lived in China, where she was taught mathematics by her father and astronomy by her grandfather. She published a paper describing lunar and solar eclipses, and by using a lamp and a mirror, demonstrated that a lunar eclipse was a scientific phenomenon, not caused by the gods as many believed.

BORN:	DIED:
1768, Jiangning, China	1797, Jiangning, China

Looking Deeper

With bigger, more powerful telescopes, astronomers could see further into the sky. And they discovered that there was a lot more out there than just stars! The French astronomer Charles Messier (1730–1817) was obsessed with searching for comets. This led him to carefully compile a catalogue of fuzzy objects in the night sky. He wanted to make comet hunting easier, by creating a list of objects that might easily be mistaken for comets.

Charles Messier

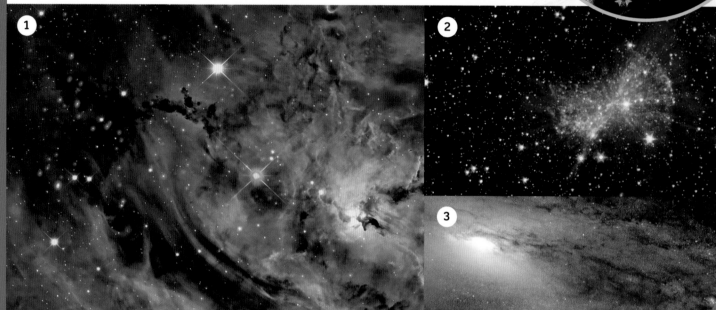

Objects in Messier's catalogue as captured by the Hubble Space Telescope: 1. Messier 8, Lagoon Nebula; 2. Messier 27, Dumbbell Nebula; 3. Messier 98, a spiral galaxy; 4. Stellar nursery NGC 604, part of Messier 33, Triangulum Galaxy; 5. Messier 75, a star cluster; 6. Messier 81, a spiral galaxy.

Messier's Catalogue

Messier called the objects in his catalogue 'nebulae' (or 'nebulas'), meaning 'clouds'. To astronomers today, a nebula is a giant cloud of dust and gas in space. These form when a giant star explodes, or are 'nurseries' where new stars are forming. Some of Messier's nebulae actually are that! Others are star clusters or galaxies. Astronomers today still refer to these objects by the number that Messier gave them, such as Messier 31 for the Andromeda Galaxy.

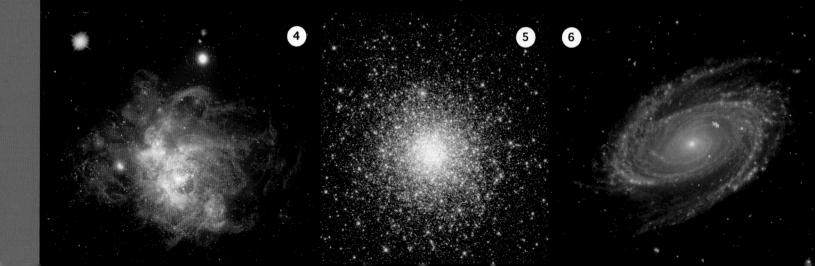

Expanding the Solar System

The discovery of Uranus in 1781 led astronomers to wonder if there were more planets out there. By studying the orbit of Uranus, they realised that it didn't move quite as they expected. There must be a large object beyond it, whose gravity was disturbing Uranus's orbit. A French maths whizz called Urbain Le Verrier made careful calculations to work out where this mystery object would have to be to cause the 'wobbles' that had been observed. He passed his results to astronomer Johann Galle. In 1846, Galle pointed his telescope as directed and found Neptune, the eighth planet in the Solar System!

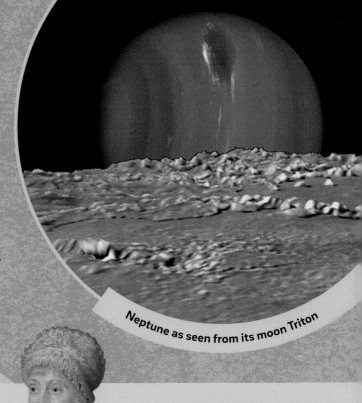

Neptune as seen from its moon Triton

Caroline Herschel

Caroline Herschel is considered the first professional female astronomer. Born in Germany, the younger sister of the astronomer William Herschel (see page 19), she moved to England and lived with her brother, assisting him in his astronomical discoveries. She went on to discover a number of nebulas and comets and became the first woman in England to be paid a salary for her scientific work.

BORN:
1750, Hanover, Holy Roman Empire
DIED:
1848, Hanover, German Confederation

A replica of Parsons' telescope

The Leviathan

In 1845, William Parsons (also known as Lord Rosse) built an enormous telescope at his estate in Ireland. Its mirror was 185 centimetres (73 in) wide, and the tube was about 16 metres (52 ft) long. This reflector, nicknamed 'Leviathan' because of its size, held the title of the world's largest telescope for over 70 years. Parsons mainly used it to re-examine the fuzzy objects catalogued by Messier and William Herschel's son, John.

Lassell's Telescopes

William Lassell (1799–1880) was a British businessman who made a fortune brewing beer, then used it to fund his hobby of astronomy. He built several large reflecting telescopes, including one on the island of Malta. He was frustrated with the cloudy weather in England, and preferred the clearer skies of the Mediterranean. Lassell's telescope was smaller than Rosse's Leviathan, but more powerful. With it, he discovered moons orbiting Neptune, Saturn and Uranus.

MODERN TELESCOPES

In its early days, astronomy was mostly conducted by rich amateurs who observed the positions and movement of objects in the sky. But by the dawn of the 20th century, a new breed of professional astronomer was taking over. These scientists – often trained in physics – wanted to discover what these objects actually were, and what they were made of. They were aided by larger telescopes and new tools such as the spectrograph, which splits light into different colours. By examining the colours, you can tell which elements make up the object that emitted the light.

CLEAR SKIES

New tools and techniques meant new telescopes. The Yerkes Observatory in Wisconsin had a refractor telescope built in 1897 with a giant 102-centimetre (40-in) lens. Unfortunately, its location at low altitude in the Midwest wasn't really ideal for astronomy. Other telescopes were built in the mountains of the western United States, where the ground was higher and the weather clearer. These included two large telescopes at the Mount Wilson Observatory in California (right), completed in 1917, and the Hale Telescope at the Palomar Observatory near San Diego, built in 1949.

TWINKLING STARS

Eventually, astronomers reached a point where making telescopes bigger didn't actually improve the images they produced. That's because the telescopes had to peer through Earth's atmosphere – the blanket of gases that surrounds our planet. We need these gases to breathe, but they get in the way when looking at the sky. They bend and distort the light from stars as it filters through the atmosphere. That's why stars appear to twinkle when we look at them.

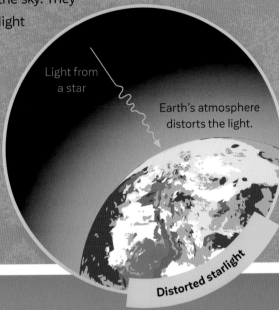

Light from a star

Earth's atmosphere distorts the light.

Distorted starlight

GETTING HIGHER

To get around the problem of the atmosphere affecting the view through a telescope, astronomers built telescopes on high mountains, where there is less of the atmosphere in the way. They also chose remote locations near oceans or deserts, where there was less light pollution, and benefitted from innovative new telescope technology designed to cancel out the blurring effect of the atmosphere. Also, as travel was becoming quicker and more efficient, astronomers were able to choose sites close to the Equator, rather than close to wherever they called home. Telescopes placed near the Equator can see a lot more stars than those placed closer to the poles.

The Mauna Kea Observatories, on Hawaii's Big Island, include large telescopes that can be moved and focused on different parts of the sky.

Other Ways to See

Stars give off light, which we can see from Earth. But they also give off energy in other forms, such as heat. Visible light is part of what we call the electromagnetic spectrum. The spectrum also includes gamma rays, X-rays, radio waves, infrared and ultraviolet. Looking for these forms of energy is a way of learning things about objects in space that we can't see with our eyes.

Gamma rays		X-rays	Ultra-violet	Infrared		Radio waves			
---	---	---	---	---	---	Radio	TV	FM	AM
0,0001 nm	0,01 nm		10 nm	1000 nm	0,01 cm	1 cm		1 m	100 m

Visible light

The difference in wavelengths along the electromagnetic spectrum in nanometres (nm), centimetres (cm) and metres (m)

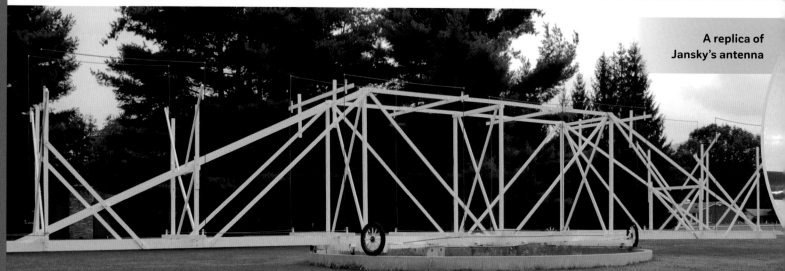

A replica of Jansky's antenna

Mysterious Static

In 1932, noisy static was interfering with short-wave radio messages being sent across the Atlantic. A young engineer called Karl Jansky, annoyed by the interference, decided to investigate. He eventually found the source of the static and tracked it for several months, discovering that it slowly shifted across the sky. With help from an astrophysicist, he realised that this source wasn't on Earth. It wasn't even in our Solar System! It came from the very heart of the Milky Way.

Karl Jansky (1905-1950)

RADIO TELESCOPES

Grote Reber (1911–2002), a radio enthusiast from the United States, read about Jansky's discovery and it inspired him to build the first radio telescope. It wasn't a tube that you look into, but rather a dish 9 metres (30 ft) wide – and it was in his back garden. He used it to survey radio waves coming from space. Soon, more powerful radio telescopes were built. They take in radio signals and use a special receiver to turn them into an image that we can see. Radio waves give us information on cold, distant stars and other objects that we wouldn't even know existed if we only used optical telescopes.

Grote Reber's antenna, built in his back garden in 1937

ACROSS THE SPECTRUM

Astronomers now have telescopes on Earth that can 'see' using various parts of the electromagnetic spectrum. There are many radio telescopes, which can make observations even if clouds are blocking the sky. Telescopes that pick up infrared radiation are rarer. They have to be placed on high mountains in dry areas, because water vapour in the atmosphere absorbs infrared. One infrared telescope, called SOFIA, flies around on a 747 plane! There is even a telescope called HESS that picks up high-energy gamma rays. But other forms of energy are blocked by Earth's atmosphere.

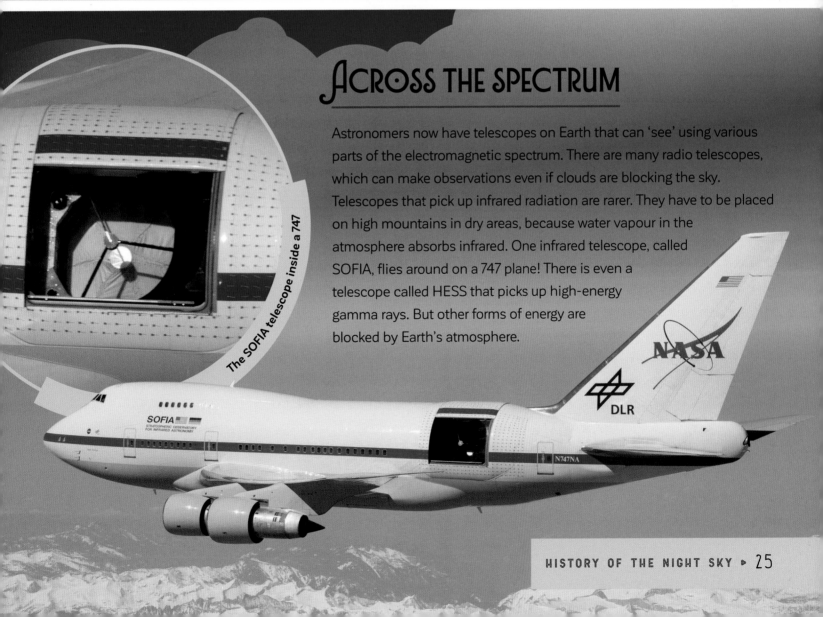

The SOFIA telescope inside a 747

THE NEXT STEP

If astronomers want a better view than ground-based telescopes can provide, they have to look at the sky from above the atmosphere. That means launching telescopes into space! A space telescope orbits the Earth, looking deep into space and sending images and information back to the ground. Today, our planet is surrounded by telescopes high in the sky.

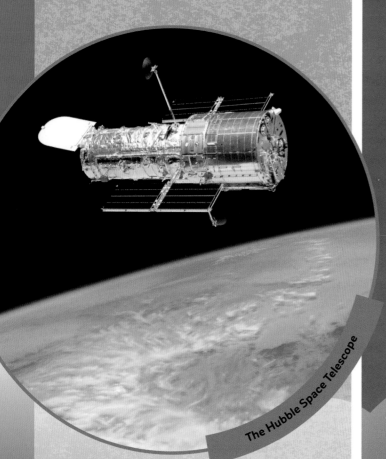

The Hubble Space Telescope

DISASTER AVERTED!

About a month after Hubble's launch (see right), astronomers discovered that its main mirror was faulty, and it was making the images fuzzy. There were also problems with the telescope's solar power and the gyroscopes that helped to position it. For a while, it looked like Hubble was going to be a multi-million-dollar disaster. But in 1993, the Space Shuttle Endeavour came to the rescue. Its astronauts conducted five spacewalks to fix the problems.

HOORAY FOR HUBBLE!

The Hubble Space Telescope was launched in 1990. It is an optical telescope that takes images in visible light, but it also has tools for detecting ultraviolet and infrared. Although it is smaller than some ground-based telescopes, Hubble's position above the atmosphere gives it a spectacular view, and it has sent back incredible images. Hubble has witnessed a comet crashing into Jupiter and found two new moons orbiting Pluto (see pages 76–77). It has helped astronomers pinpoint the age of the Universe and taken photos of thousands of galaxies in deep space.

One of the remarkable images captured by the Hubble Space Telescope, this shows the 'Pillars of Creation' – giant towers of gas and dust where new stars are born, part of the Eagle Nebula.

TELESCOPES IN THE SKY

Space is full of microwave radiation left over from the Big Bang when the Universe began. Space telescopes, like the Cosmic Background Explorer (COBE) launched by the US space agency NASA in 1989, help astronomers measure this radiation. The Planck observatory, launched by the European Space Agency (ESA) in 2009, continued that work. In 2003, NASA launched the Spitzer Space Telescope to pick up infrared radiation. In the same year, NASA also sent up the Galaxy Evolution Explorer (GALEX satellite), which focused on ultraviolet radiation.

The Spitzer Space Telescope

The Chandra X-ray Observatory

HIGH ENERGY

Detecting X-rays and gamma rays is difficult because they are small and energetic. They don't bounce off a mirror like visible light does – they pass through it! Astronomers can learn a lot from X-rays and gamma rays, but telescopes must be designed carefully to detect them. The Chandra X-ray Observatory, taken into orbit in 1999, flies high above the Earth. It has been used to study quasars, black holes and supernovas. It has even witnessed galaxies colliding with each other!

EXPLORING THE SKIES

Professional astronomers get to play with some very impressive toys, but their job takes years of training and study. However, astronomy doesn't have to be a job – it can be a fascinating hobby as well! Around the world, amateur astronomers just like you are exploring the skies.

The Crab Nebula, in the constellation of Taurus, is the remains of an exploded star.

Saturn's rings seen through an 11-inch telescope

Amazing amateurs

You don't need a giant telescope to see some pretty amazing things. In fact, a pair of simple binoculars can open up whole new worlds! You can see craters and detail on the surface of the Moon. And with a small telescope, you'll see even more – including Saturn's rings. Even if all you have is your eyes, you can spot constellations and follow them across the sky. With limited equipment, amateur astronomers have made some impressive discoveries. In 2016, a locksmith in Argentina was lucky enough to catch the first moments of a spectacular supernova – the enormous explosion that marks the end of a massive star. Other amateurs have discovered new comets and nebulas, and have even spotted an asteroid crashing into Jupiter.

So who knows? The next discovery could come from you! And even if it doesn't, stargazing is still a great way to learn more about space.

SEEING CLEARLY

You probably already know about the pollution of water and air, thanks to chemicals and rubbish. But did you know that light can pollute too? Our towns and cities rely on electric lights, and many of these stay on throughout the night. The light they produce brightens the night sky, making it hard to see all but the brightest stars.

ESCAPE TO THE COUNTRY

If you live in a city, don't worry – you'll still be able to see a bit. But if you can get out into the countryside, you'll be amazed at the difference. Choose a night with no clouds and no Moon, and a whole new world will open up. You'll see multitudes of stars, and possibly even the glorious sweep of the Milky Way arcing across the sky.

Looking at the Earth from above, you can see the concentration of light in the cities. It can be easier to see the night sky away from these centres.

WHAT TO USE

You can see a lot through a pair of binoculars.

You don't necessarily need a telescope to be a stargazer. In fact, you can see a lot with the naked eye. A pair of binoculars, though, will help you see even more, and is a relatively inexpensive first step to take. Binoculars work by collecting more light than your eyes can, which lets you see faint objects that you wouldn't see otherwise. They also magnify and make the objects look bigger. Binoculars are marked with a pair of numbers, like 10 × 50. The first number shows how much they magnify, so a 10 means that an object will look ten times bigger than with the naked eye. The second number gives the diameter, in millimetres, of the larger pair of lenses. The bigger the lenses, the more light they collect – though they do get heavy and harder to hold steady. Anything above 50 is probably heavy enough to require a tripod.

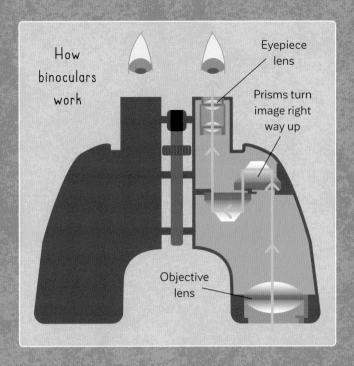

How binoculars work

Eyepiece lens

Prisms turn image right way up

Objective lens

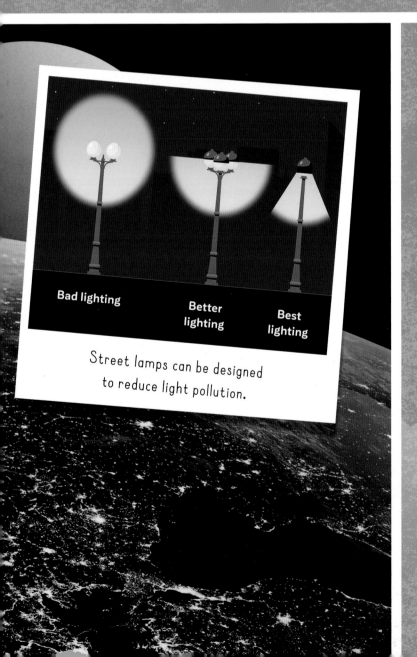

Bad lighting

Better lighting

Best lighting

Street lamps can be designed to reduce light pollution.

SPOTTING SCOPES

A spotting scope is compact and easy to use, like a pair of binoculars, but it has a single eyepiece like a telescope. Though most models are designed for birdwatchers and hunters, they are also useful for looking at the sky. Spotting scopes are generally tough and rugged, and they are easier for a beginner to use than a telescope. Many scopes can magnify up to 60 times, with a zoom eyepiece that lets you focus in on your target once you've found it. You will need to mount the scope on a tripod to keep it steady at higher magnifications.

A spotting scope

Your First Telescope

You've decided that stargazing is the hobby for you, and it's time to invest in a telescope. But there are a lot of options, and a lot of very technical-sounding terms. Even beginner telescopes aren't cheap, so you want to make sure that you're spending your money wisely. So how do you choose?

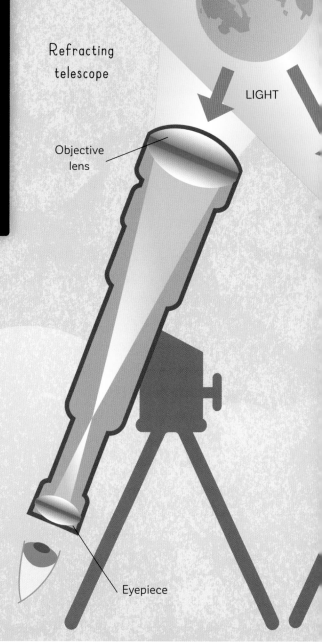

Refracting telescope

LIGHT

Objective lens

Eyepiece

Reflecting and Refracting

The two main types of telescopes are refractors and reflectors. Both are designed to take the light from a big area of the sky and get it to the small area that is your eye. Refracting telescopes do this with curved lenses. Reflecting telescopes use curved mirrors instead. A compound telescope uses a combination of mirrors and lenses.

When people talk about telescopes, they'll often use words like Newtonian, Dobsonian or Cassegrain. It may sound like gibberish, but these are just different styles of telescope. Each one has the mirrors and lenses laid out in a slightly different way. They are named after the people who invented or designed them – like Isaac Newton in the case of the Newtonian telescope.

Holding Steady

Unlike binoculars or a spotting scope, which you can hold in your hands, a telescope needs a mount (pictured right). The mount holds the telescope steady and allows you to point it in different directions. A mount that is described as 'altitude-azimuth' means that the telescope can move side to side as well as up and down. A more complicated mount called an equatorial has a rotational axis that is parallel to Earth's axis of rotation. Using this kind of mount can help your telescope track the stars across the sky as the Earth rotates. Some equatorial mounts even have a motor to do this automatically!

EYEPIECES AND FINDER SCOPES

Reflecting telescope

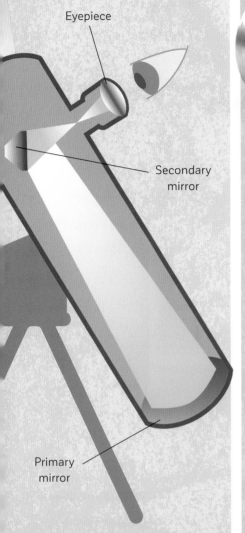

Eyepiece

Secondary mirror

Primary mirror

An eyepiece

Every telescope has an eyepiece – the part that you actually look through. It contains the final lens that passes light on to your eye. Most telescopes have several eyepieces you can swap out, each with a different magnification. The bigger the magnification, the more detail you'll see, but it means focusing on a smaller area of the sky.

In fact, telescopes focus on such a small area that even if you can see something with your eyes, getting it into the telescope's field of view can be fiddly. That's why many telescopes come with a finder scope! This is basically a small telescope attached to the main one, with both pointing in the exact same direction. The finder scope is less powerful, but it covers a larger area of the sky. You use it to find your target, then swap to the main telescope to examine the target more closely.

A finder scope on a refracting telescope

TRY BEFORE YOU BUY

Is there a local astronomy club in your area? Tag along to one of their meetings. You'll have a chance to try out different types of telescopes and get advice as to which one is right for you.

CHANGING VIEWS

One of the reasons why stargazing is such a fascinating hobby is that no two nights are quite the same. There's the weather to contend with, of course, but the view is also constantly changing. Stars and planets and moons don't stay still, and Earth's spinning on its axis means that the piece of the sky you are looking at alters all the time.

MOVING STARS

Imagine that you spotted a constellation one evening just after the Sun went down. But before you could have a proper look, you got called in to supper. You make it back out a few hours later, with a flask of hot cocoa at the ready, and look up in the same spot, but the constellation isn't there! Where did it go?

Phew! Before long, you spot it, just a bit northwest of where it had been before. And the explanation for why it moved is really simple. On Earth, we experience day and night because our planet rotates (spins around) a full turn each day. This makes the Sun appear to rise in the east, move across the sky, and then set in the west. And that's what many stars do at night!

The star group known as the Plough seen just above the horizon

POLE STARS

The stars that lie more or less directly above the North and South Poles do not seem to move at all. If you were standing at the North Pole, Polaris (also called the Pole Star) would be directly overhead. From other locations in the Northern Hemisphere, you look north to spot it. It stays still while the other stars rotate anticlockwise around it. In the Southern Hemisphere, Sigma Octantis appears high in the southern sky. The other stars rotate clockwise around it.

KNOW YOUR PLACE

The skies change with the seasons, too, with constellations moving around and some disappearing entirely. This is to do with the yearly path that Earth takes around the Sun. Remember that at night, you'll be on the side of Earth facing away from the Sun. So in the summer you're looking at a completely different patch of the galaxy than you are in the winter. Some constellations will be visible all year round, while others will disappear for months at a time.

Before any stargazing expedition, you'll need to know which constellations are visible in the current season. A stargazing book like this one can help with that, and there are also some really great stargazing apps available. Once you've got a target in mind, you'll also need to know which direction to look, and how high above the horizon it will be. Star maps will tell you whether a constellation appears in the north, south, east or west, as well as its altitude.

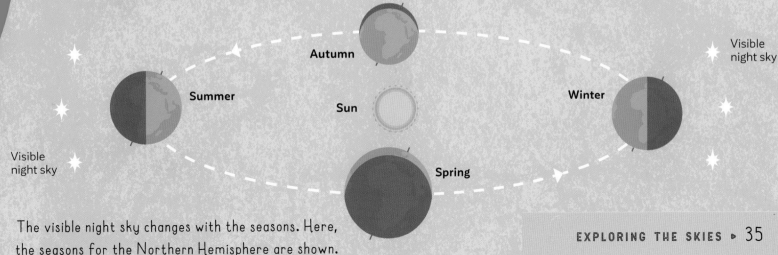

The visible night sky changes with the seasons. Here, the seasons for the Northern Hemisphere are shown.

STARGAZING SURVIVAL KIT

You've picked a location, the Sun has set, and it's finally time for your stargazing expedition. But it's best to be prepared! Here is a checklist of things that you'll need to take with you.

+ Don't go out at night on your own – take a responsible adult with you. Who knows, they may also be useful when it comes to helping you find objects in the sky!

+ It probably goes without saying, but don't forget your telescope or binoculars.

+ Once the Sun goes down, the temperature drops, and in some places it will likely be colder than you expect. Wearing layers is a great idea – you can take them on or off as the temperature changes.

+ You might be out there for a while! Pack a drink and some snacks in your rucksack.

+ Standing and tilting your head back is a great way to get a sore neck! If you can, take a folding chair or sun lounger you can lie on to get a great view without straining your neck. You can also take a blanket to lie on the ground, but this can get pretty chilly in cold weather.

+ Take a torch or headlamp and cover the bulb with see-through red plastic (or use a red bike light). It takes about half an hour for your eyes to get fully adjusted to the dark, allowing you to see fainter objects in the sky. If you flick on a torch or look at a phone screen, you'll have to wait for your eyes to adjust once more. When light goes through a red filter, it doesn't spoil your night vision.

+ You'll definitely need a guide to the skies, like this book. You can also get brilliant apps for a phone or tablet that help you find objects in the sky. Some of them use the device's sensors, so you can point them at an area of sky and they'll tell you what you're looking at. Some devices and apps have a red-screen option that lets you use them without spoiling your night vision.

And that's it! So with your bag packed and your responsible adult in tow, it's time to head out. Next stop, the Milky Way ...

Snacks ☐

Drinks ☐

Headlamp ☐

Torch ☐

Binoculars ☐

Warm clothes ☐

Folding chair ☐

NAVIGATING THE SKY

Imagine that you're lost in a forest. There are trees in every direction you turn, and they all look more or less the same. It's just a thick, patternless mass, and you're not even sure which direction you're facing. Looking at the night sky can feel a bit like this, especially if there are a lot of stars visible. At first glance, it looks like a random, disordered sprinkling. However, if you can spot landmark trees in a forest, you can use them to find your way round. You can use stars in the same way.

Both trees and stars can be used to guide you when you're lost.

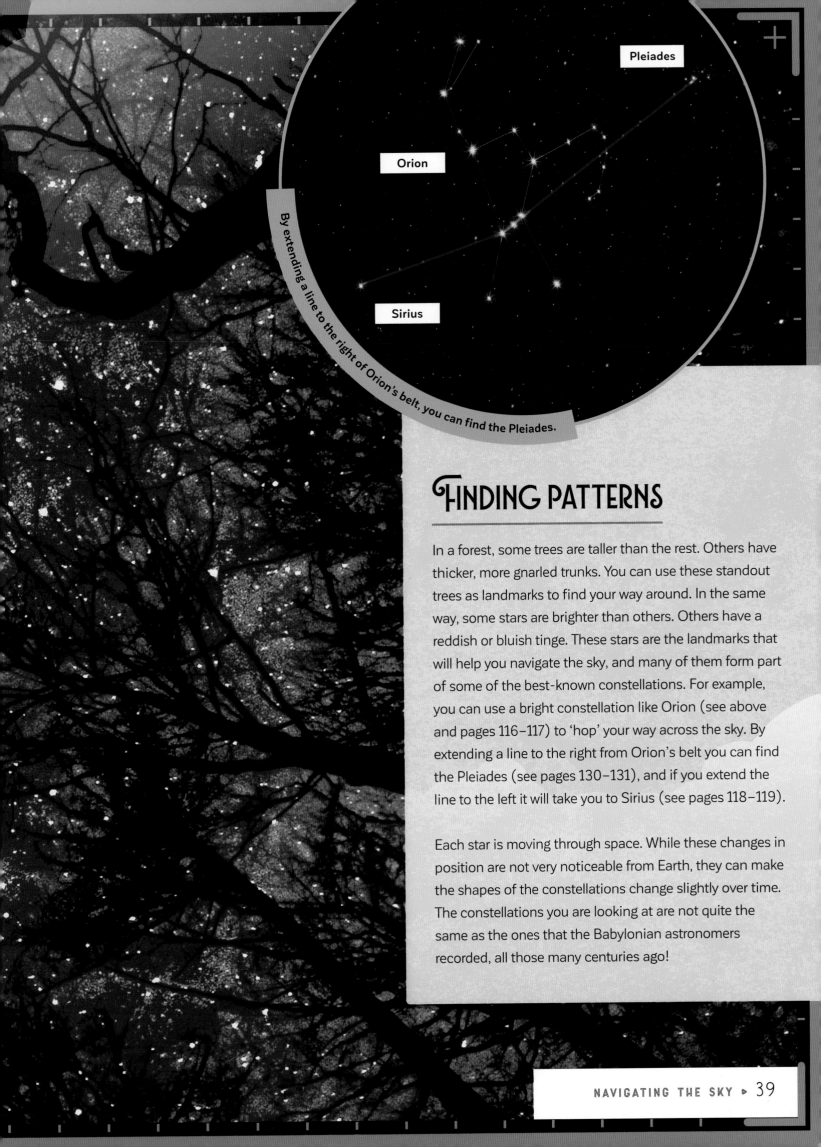

Pleiades

Orion

Sirius

By extending a line to the right of Orion's belt, you can find the Pleiades.

FINDING PATTERNS

In a forest, some trees are taller than the rest. Others have thicker, more gnarled trunks. You can use these standout trees as landmarks to find your way around. In the same way, some stars are brighter than others. Others have a reddish or bluish tinge. These stars are the landmarks that will help you navigate the sky, and many of them form part of some of the best-known constellations. For example, you can use a bright constellation like Orion (see above and pages 116–117) to 'hop' your way across the sky. By extending a line to the right from Orion's belt you can find the Pleiades (see pages 130–131), and if you extend the line to the left it will take you to Sirius (see pages 118–119).

Each star is moving through space. While these changes in position are not very noticeable from Earth, they can make the shapes of the constellations change slightly over time. The constellations you are looking at are not quite the same as the ones that the Babylonian astronomers recorded, all those many centuries ago!

A WORLD OF TWO HALVES

These days, it's easy to connect with people all over the world. You may have friends in different countries, and some of them might even share your hobby of stargazing. But even though you have that in common, there's one important difference – you may be looking at completely different stars!

New York, USA

Santiago, Chile

BACK TO BASICS

To understand how people across the world can be gazing at different stars, think about the Earth and its position in space. Our planet is a sphere with an imaginary line going right through it, from the North Pole to the South Pole. Earth rotates around this line, known as the axis, at a slight angle (called axial tilt) to create night and day, as one side passes in and then out of the Sun's light.

Midway between the two poles there is another imaginary line, this one circling the Earth like a belt. It's called the Equator. The half of the planet that sits north of the Equator is the Northern Hemisphere, and the half to the south is the Southern Hemisphere.

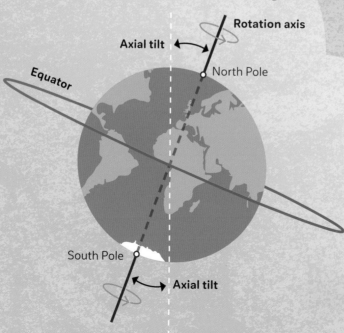

Rotation axis

Axial tilt

Equator

North Pole

South Pole

Axial tilt

The Southern Hemisphere constellation Crux can be seen from parts of the Northern Hemisphere.

A TALE OF TWO CITIES

New York (left) is more or less due north from Santiago, Chile (bottom left). New York is in the Northern Hemisphere and Santiago is in the Southern Hemisphere. Although there are differences between the exact sunrise and sunset times, the two cities have day and night at pretty much the same time. But their seasons are opposite – when it is summer in New York, it is winter in Santiago. On the other side of the world, Beijing and Perth also have similar day and night but opposite seasons.

Earth's celestial sphere

Astronomers in the Northern and Southern Hemispheres also see different stars. Imagine the rest of the Universe as a hollow sphere surrounding the Earth. Our planet is at the centre, and there are stars in all directions around it. Wherever you stand on Earth, you can see half of this 'celestial sphere'. The other half is below the horizon – it's effectively blocked by the rest of the planet. Someone standing in the opposite hemisphere, though, can see the stars that you can't.

SHARING STARS

There are some stars and constellations that are only ever visible from the northern part of the planet. Likewise, there are some that are only visible from the southern part. But there are quite a few that are visible from both, sometimes at different times of year. And the closer you are to the Equator, the more of the other hemisphere's constellations you'll be able to see.

MOVING THROUGH SPACE

It's easy to see why people in the past thought that Earth stood still while the Sun, Moon and stars travelled around it. After all, when you stand on the ground, it doesn't feel like it's moving. You can't feel Earth spinning or zooming through space as it travels around the Sun. Instead, you see the Sun rising and setting over the course of the day, and constellations rising and setting at night. It gives the impression that all these objects are attached to an invisible celestial sphere, which is slowly rotating around a stationary Earth.

NICOLAUS COPERNICUS

Nicolaus Copernicus was a Polish astronomer who lived at a time when pretty much everyone believed that Earth was the centre of the Universe. This idea certainly had its problems – planets often appeared to travel backwards, which some astronomers explained by suggesting complicated, looping paths for them. Copernicus worked out that it all made much more sense if the Sun was at the centre, and Earth and everything else travelled around it.

BORN:
1473, Thorn, Royal Prussia, Poland

DIED:
1543, Frauenburg, Royal Prussia, Poland

Ecliptic

The ecliptic is the path the Sun seems to take across the sky.

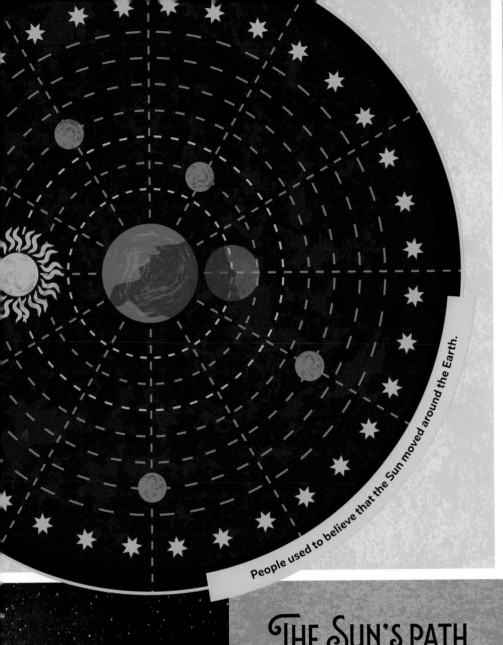

People used to believe that the Sun moved around the Earth.

☉N THE MOVE

The stars always appear to stay more or less in the same positions relative to each other – that is to say, the shapes of the constellations don't really change. But the Sun is the exception to this rule. It appears to move across the celestial sphere. Relative to the stars, the Sun shifts a little bit each day, and after a year it's back where it started. This is hard to see, of course, because the Sun appears during the day and the constellations appear at night. But the constellations are always there, even during the day when their light is drowned out by the Sun's. So if you know the pattern of how they move, you know which constellation is behind the Sun at any given time – even if you can't actually see it.

The Sun's Path

The path that the Sun appears to take is called the ecliptic. The Moon and planets seem to follow this path, too. That's because of the way the Solar System is arranged, with the Sun at the centre and the planets travelling in a flat disc around it like the brim of a hat. The ecliptic is marked on many star maps, and it's useful to know where it is, because it will help you find planets in the night sky.

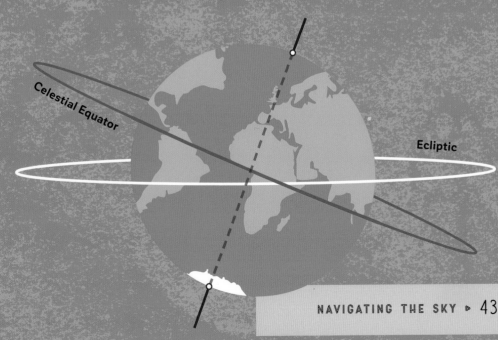

Celestial Equator

Ecliptic

Distances and Degrees

Many ancient peoples thought that the stars were all the same distance away and fixed to a single sphere. We now know that, although the stars are all incredibly far away from us, some are much, much further than others. But the ancient idea of a 'celestial sphere' (see page 41) is still a useful image to keep in your head. Seeing the skies as a dome above you makes it easier to use geometry to find your way around.

How Far?

When you're trying to use one star to find another, it doesn't matter how far apart they actually are in space. What does matter is how far from each other they appear on the celestial sphere. And we measure this distance in degrees. It's rather similar to the way we use degrees of latitude and longitude to pinpoint a location on Earth's surface.

This telescope is looking out from an observatory.

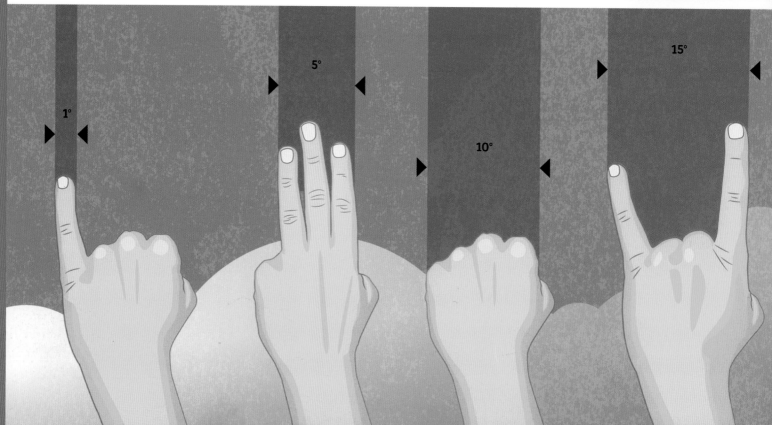

1° 5° 10° 15°

Azimuth and Altitude

Imagine the skies above you as being half of a sphere. The horizon, where this hemisphere meets the ground, forms a circle. The circle is divided into 360 equal segments called degrees. These degrees are used to pinpoint an object's azimuth (its direction along the horizon, in relation to the compass points). Azimuth references start at 0 degrees at due north and move around clockwise. Now imagine a line going from the top of your head to the top of the hemisphere. Where they meet is called the zenith. Your body is at a right angle to the ground, so there are 90 degrees from the horizon up to the zenith. The measurement of a star's altitude can be found by estimating the angle from the ground to the star. Below is the position of a star with an azimuth of 120° and an altitude of 45°.

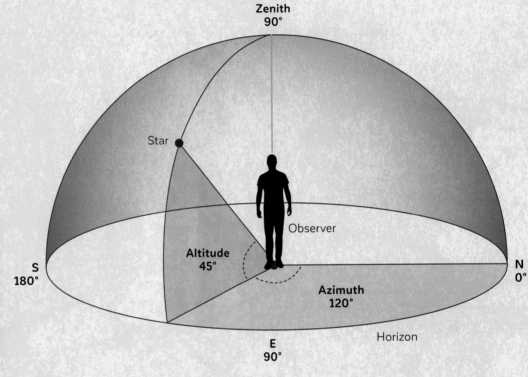

Zenith
90°

Star

Observer

Altitude
45°

S
180°

N
0°

Azimuth
120°

E
90°

Horizon

Where am I?

Azimuth and altitude can be tricky to use. That's partly because the stars move over the course of the night, and also because their coordinates will be different for two people in different locations. Degrees are most useful for using a star that you recognise to find another. If you know how many degrees apart they are, you can estimate that using your hand. Stand with your arm stretched out and point it at the first star, with your hand closed into a fist. The distance from one side of your fist to the other is about 10 degrees. If you stick up your index and little finger to make the 'rock on!' sign, that will be about 15 degrees. It's not exact, but using your hand can help you to estimate these distances. You can also picture the full Moon, which is about half a degree across.

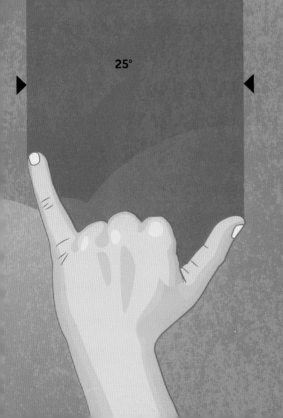

25°

STAR MAPS

To find your way on Earth, you pretty much need only one map. The continents don't move (at least, not enough to make any difference), and cities stay in the same spot all year round. But when it comes to maps of the sky, it's a bit more complicated …

STAR MAPS ARE SPECIAL

Star maps are usually round. The outer rim represents the horizon, and the centre represents the zenith (see pages 44–45). So an object that appears halfway between the centre and the edge will be about halfway up the sky. Another thing that you'll notice about star maps is that the compass directions look like they're the wrong way round. If you compare one to what you can actually see in the sky, it seems like the 'east' and 'west' markings are swapped. But remember that it's a map of the sky, not the ground. If you hold it over your head, facing down, they'll be the right way round!

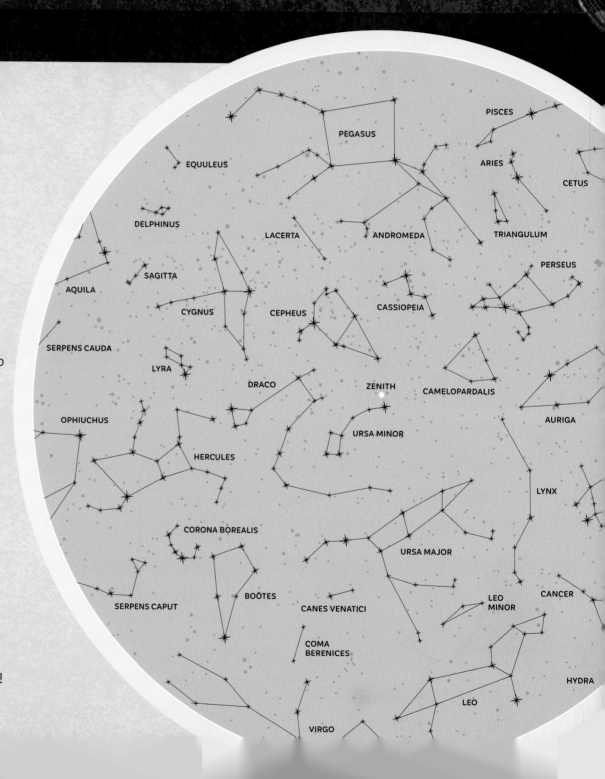

How Many Maps?

For stargazing, you'll need the right map. It needs to show the correct hemisphere, for a start! The time of year matters too, as well as whether you're looking in the evening or the morning. Some guides have a series of maps, one for each season. You can also use a planisphere or 'star wheel', such as the one on the left. This is a simple device with a spinning dial. You spin it to set the current time and date, and the viewing window shows the visible stars.

Magnitude

Astronomers use a measurement called apparent magnitude to measure how bright a star appears to viewers on Earth. The smaller the number, the brighter the star. So Sirius, with an apparent magnitude of –1.44, looks brighter than Regulus, with an apparent magnitude of 1.36. On star maps, brighter objects are often shown as larger dots, to make them easier to spot.

Star maps showing the major constellations in the Northern Hemisphere (left) and Southern Hemisphere (right). See pages 94–127.

The Andromeda Galaxy is a stunning
sight through a powerful telescope.

WHAT TO SEE

At last, you're ready. You know your altitude from your
azimuth, your ecliptic from your Equator, your reflector from your
refractor. It's time to take all this knowledge and turn your gaze to
the heavens. But what will you see?

Stars, obviously – lots and lots of stars! As you find your way around the
sky, you'll see them start to form shapes and patterns, and you'll also see
how some are brighter or have faint colours. But you'll also spot planets,
which look enough like stars to fool the casual observer. With the right
equipment, you'll even see moons orbiting some of them.

Shooting stars are burning rocks falling through Earth's atmosphere.

Near and Far

Planets and moons are close to home, astronomically speaking. The stars are further away, but they're still within our own galaxy. Look in the right place, though, and you'll see distant galaxies. Observing them is like taking a trip back in time. The Andromeda Galaxy (see page 148), for example, is so far away that the light from its stars takes 2,540,000 years to reach us. When you see it, you're looking at a snapshot of the galaxy as it was more than two and a half million years ago.

Let's start the journey a bit closer to home though, with the biggest and brightest object in the sky...

THE SUN

It's ironic that the most obvious object in the sky is also the one that you should never look at directly. The Sun is bright and beautiful, but its light is so intense that it can damage your eyes. Luckily, having to avoid looking at it doesn't mean that you can't learn some interesting facts about it!

A close-up of the Sun's surface shows that it is swirling with activity.

What is the Sun?

The Sun is a star, just like the many others that you see in the sky. It only looks different because it is so much closer to us than the rest of the stars. A few ancient astronomers, such as the Greek philosopher Anaxagoras, who lived in Athens in the 5th century BCE, suspected that the Sun and the stars were the same thing. However, this wasn't finally proved until the 1800s. We know now that the Sun is really just a normal, medium-sized star.

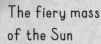

The fiery mass of the Sun

Cecilia Payne-Gaposchkin

Cecilia Payne was born in England, but she moved to the USA in the 1920s to do a doctoral thesis at Harvard University. At this time, most astronomers believed that the Sun and other stars were made up of a similar mix of elements that are found in Earth's crust. But Payne studied the colours of light coming out of the Sun using spectroscopy and discovered that it was made mainly of hydrogen and helium, with small amounts of the other elements. Her discovery changed our fundamental understanding about stars.

BORN:	DIED:
1900, Wendover, England	1979, Massachusetts, United States

INSIDE THE SUN

Although Anaxagoras thought that the Sun was a fiery stone, it's actually a ball of super-hot gas. Like all stars, it's made up mostly of hydrogen and helium. Deep inside its core, a nuclear reaction takes place that fuses hydrogen atoms to form helium. This process releases a huge amount of energy. Some of it reaches our planet in the form of heat and light.

Energy travels from the core through the Sun and out into space.

Core: where nuclear reactions take place

Corona: fiery aura surrounding the Sun

Sunspot: cooler area on surface

Photosphere: visible 'surface' of the Sun

SOLAR ECLIPSE

The Sun is about 400 times as wide as the Moon, but it is also about 400 times further away. This lucky coincidence means that they appear almost exactly the same size in the sky. When they line up exactly, the Moon can completely block the Sun. This is called a solar eclipse (left). These eerie occurrences make the skies darken in the middle of the day. But remember – even during the low light of an eclipse, it is still not safe to look at the Sun.

THE MOON

When you're listing the brightest objects in the sky, the Moon comes in at number two. It's our nearest neighbour in space, and it's the only body that humans have visited. It's also completely fascinating to look at and study!

IMPACT!

The Moon is solid and rocky, like the Earth, but the similarities end there. The Moon has practically zero atmosphere, and no liquid water on the surface. The ground is pitted with craters left by comets and asteroids crashing into it, such as the one shown above. The faint trace of an atmosphere is too thin to protect the Moon from impacts, and with no wind or water to wear away the craters, they stay for billions of years.

Mare Crisium is a lunar 'sea' that is easily visible from Earth.

☉N THE SURFACE

The Moon's surface is mainly made up of grey, powdery dust and rocks. The lighter areas are highlands. The dark patches that you can see from Earth are large impact basins that were filled with lava long ago, back when the Moon still had active volcanoes. They are called *maria*, which is Latin for 'seas'.

Katherine Johnson

Before NASA had electronic computers to crank out calculations, they used 'human computers' instead. Katherine Johnson was one of these, although as an African American woman, she had to overcome many obstacles during her career. She used her mathematical genius to help calculate the flight paths for some of NASA's first missions, including the Apollo 11 mission that took astronauts to the moon.

BORN:
1918, West Virginia, United States

DIED:
2020, Virginia, United States

THE FAR SIDE

The far side of the Moon

From Earth, the features of the Moon always look pretty much the same – that's because we only ever see one side of the Moon. It takes the Moon the same amount of time to travel around the Earth – about 27 days – as it does to rotate once. This means that the same side of it is always facing towards us. Thanks to a 'wobble' in the Moon's movement, called libration, over the course of the month we can actually see about 59 per cent of the Moon's surface. Our first glimpse of the far side came in 1959, when the Soviet Luna 3 spacecraft went around and sent photos back. It is more rugged than the near side, with many craters.

CHANGING SHAPE

One of the most obvious things you'll notice about the Moon is that it doesn't always look the same. Sometimes it's a full disc, other times it's a semicircle, and a few days a month it's a thin crescent. What gives?

REFLECTED LIGHT

The Sun is bright because it makes its own light. The Moon can't do this, though. Instead, it reflects the Sun's light. At any given moment, the half of the Moon that is facing the Sun is lit up, and the other half is dark. Depending on where the Moon is on its monthly journey around Earth, we can see a different portion of the lit-up side.

The Moon is sometimes visible during the day.

PHASES

Over the course of 29.5 days, the Moon goes through a series of phases (below). Starting with a new Moon, it gradually grows (or waxes) to a crescent shape and then to a semicircle and up to a full Moon. Then it shrinks (or wanes) down to a semicircle and then to a crescent until it appears as a new Moon again. Humans have been tracking these phases for thousands of years, and they have used them to mark the passage of time. In fact, the word 'month' comes from 'Moon'!

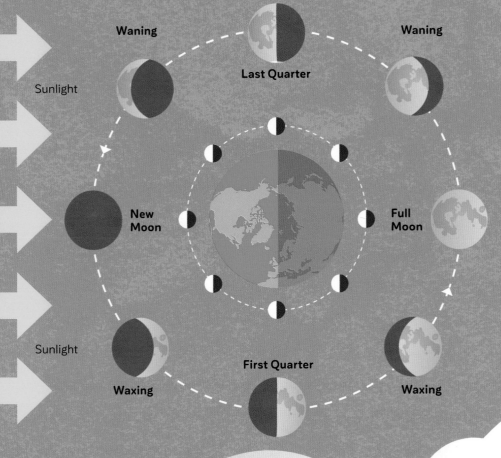

Waning

Sunlight

Last Quarter

Waning

New Moon

Full Moon

Sunlight

First Quarter

Waxing

Waxing

EARTHSHINE

You may have noticed that even when the Moon is a crescent, you can sometimes still see the whole Moon, with the darkened portion glowing very faintly. Just as the Moon reflects light from the Sun, so does the Earth. Our reflected light is what's illuminating the darkened part of the Moon. Astronomers call this 'earthshine'. And if you were standing on the surface of the moon, you'd see a nearly 'full Earth' glowing brightly in the night sky.

'Earthshine'

UP OR DOWN?

We often think of the Moon as the opposite of the Sun – the Sun rules the daytime skies and the Moon rules the night. But, in fact, the Moon is often visible during the day, and sometimes at night it disappears!

Earth's rotation makes the Moon rise more or less in the east and set more or less in the west, just like the Sun. Each day, the Moon rises about 50 minutes later than the day before. This pattern means that sometimes the Moon is rising during the day. And because it is so near and so bright, the Sun's light can't quite drown it out, like it does with the light from the stars. So there you have it – the amazing daytime Moon!

A lunar eclipse happens when the Earth covers part or all of the Moon, throwing it into shadow.

LUNAR ECLIPSES

In a solar eclipse (see pages 50–51), the Moon passes directly between the Sun and the Earth, blocking the Sun's light. In a lunar eclipse, it's more or less the same, except that the positions have swapped. Earth travels between the Sun and Moon, blocking the light and casting a shadow that throws the Moon into darkness. But although Earth passes between the Sun and Moon every month, lunar eclipses happen just a few times a year. That's because the Moon's orbit is tilted, so it often passes above or below Earth's shadow. Eclipses only happen when the Moon and Earth line up perfectly.

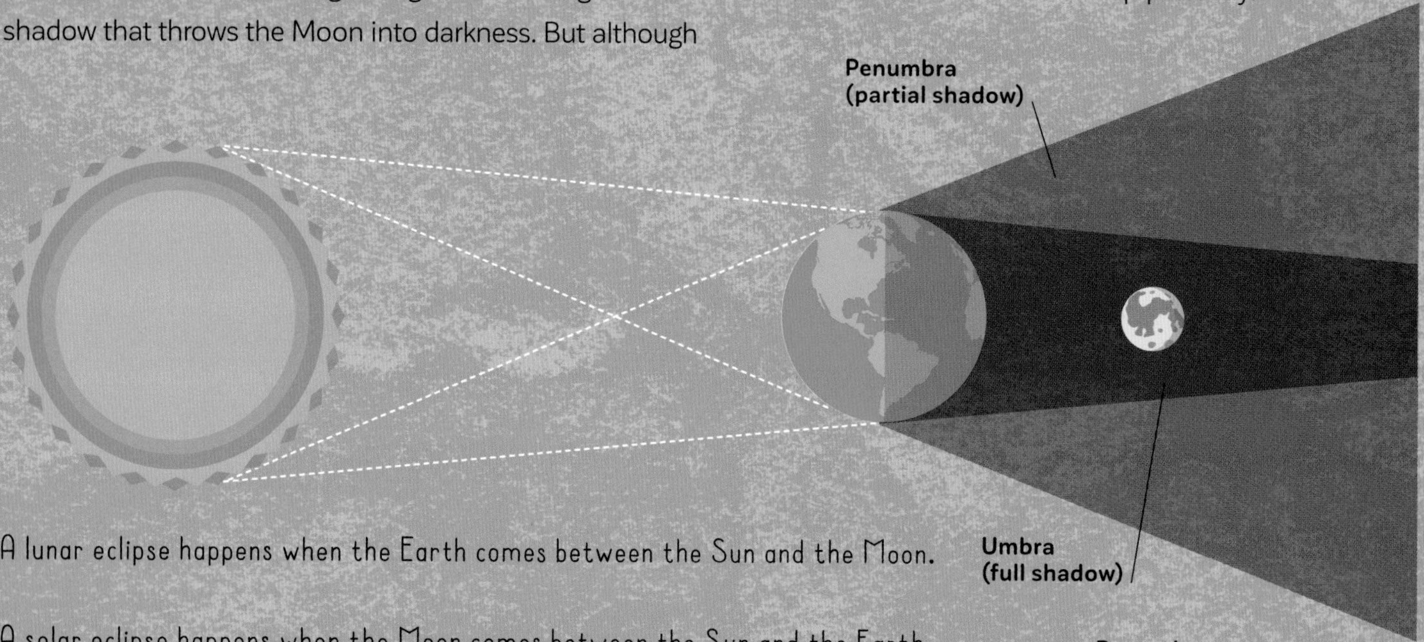

Penumbra (partial shadow)

Umbra (full shadow)

A lunar eclipse happens when the Earth comes between the Sun and the Moon.

A solar eclipse happens when the Moon comes between the Sun and the Earth.

Penumbra

Umbra

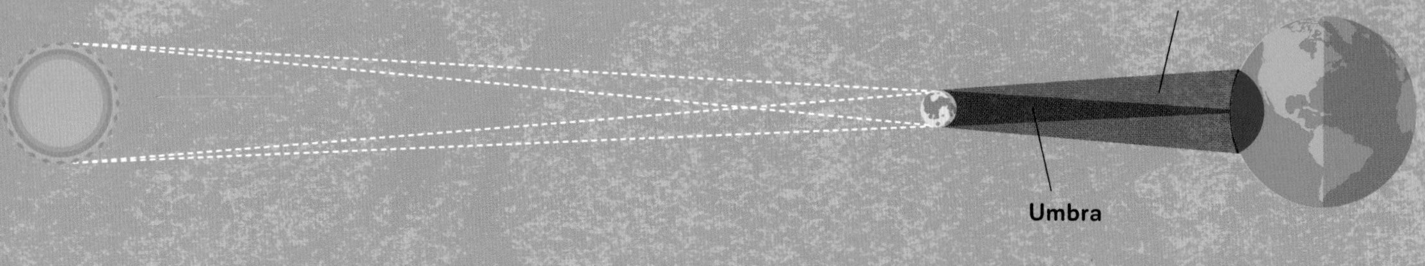

Blood Moon

During an eclipse, Earth's shadow appears to take a crescent-shaped 'bite' out of the Moon, which grows as the shadow covers more of the Moon. Eventually the whole thing is covered by Earth's shadow, called the umbra. Instead of disappearing, the Moon sometimes turns red – an event known as a 'blood Moon' (right). It can also turn orange or grey, depending on the weather on Earth. This may look scary and ominous, but it has a perfectly logical scientific explanation. Earth's atmosphere scatters blue light, sending it out into space, while it bends the red light and focuses it on the Moon.

Eclipse Legends

There are plenty of myths and stories that have tried to explain what happens during a lunar eclipse. To the Inca people who lived in South America in the 1400s and 1500s, the red colour meant that a jaguar was attacking the Moon. To protect the Earth, they would shake their spears and make a fearsome noise. In ancient Mesopotamia (from around 4000 BCE), an eclipse meant the king was in danger from demons. The Mesopotamian people knew enough about astronomy to predict eclipses, so when one was coming, they put a fake king on the throne and sent the real one into hiding.

Inca people shook spears at the Moon.

Helping the Moon

Other eclipse legends are less scary. One of the indigenous peoples of California, the Luiseño, believed that an eclipse showed that the Moon was wounded or ill. To heal it, they would sing and chant. The Batammaliba people, who live in Togo and Benin, see a lunar eclipse as a fight between the Sun and the Moon. Their job, as they see it, is to stop the fight, so as a people they come together to end feuds and make peace with their enemies.

Aglaonice

To ancient peoples who believed that the skies were full of gods, eclipses were seen as dark magic. Writers from ancient Greece tell of a sorceress called Aglaonice who could make the Moon disappear from the sky. She and her followers were known as the 'witches of Thessaly'. However, Aglaonice was no witch at all – she was an astronomer. She watched the skies, kept records, and could predict when a lunar eclipse would occur.

BORN:	DIED:
around 200 BCE	unknown

THE SOLAR SYSTEM

Sun

Venus   Mars

Mercury   Earth

On Earth, we are part of a very special 'family' – a family of planets! Our home is just one of eight planets that make up the Solar System. Ancient people knew about five of the other planets because they are easily visible with the naked eye. Uranus is also just visible, as long as you have good eyesight and dark skies, and know exactly where to look. To see Neptune – the furthest planet – you'll need a telescope.

Star Systems

The Solar System is our home, but it's not unique. In recent years, astronomers have discovered that many other stars have planets orbiting them. These planets are called exoplanets, and these exoplanet 'families' are called star systems, not solar systems. The word 'solar' comes from Sol, our Sun's official name, so it is only used to refer to our own system.

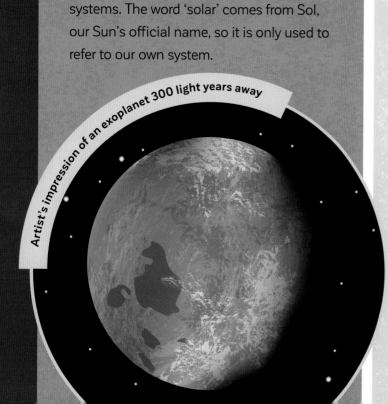

Artist's impression of an exoplanet 300 light years away

Mercury

Mercury (right) is the smallest planet in the Solar System, and also the closest to the Sun. It is a rocky world with a surface covered in craters and cliffs that were formed when the planet shrank as it cooled. There is no atmosphere thick enough to trap heat, so while it is scorching hot during the day, it is freezing at night. Mercury moves quickly through space, taking only 88 days to loop around the Sun. That's why it was named after the Roman god Mercury, a fleet-footed messenger with winged sandals.

Mercury is close enough and bright enough to see with the naked eye, but it doesn't make its own light. From our perspective, Mercury is always near the Sun. That makes it difficult to spot, because it rises and sets while the sky is still fairly light. It is always fairly close to the horizon, and the further you are from the Equator, the harder it is to see.

Asteroid
Belt

Saturn

Neptune

Uranus

Jupiter

MORE THAN PLANETS

The Solar System (shown here) is more than just planets. Everything that is affected by the Sun's gravity is part of the Solar System. This includes dozens of moons, several dwarf planets (with more still likely to be found), and millions of asteroids, comets, and small space rocks called meteoroids. Beyond Neptune, there is a ring of icy objects called the Kuiper Belt. And beyond that lies the Oort Cloud – a sphere of comets and other small bodies.

Mercury regularly passes directly between Earth and the Sun. On rare occasions – about 13 times per century – the three objects line up just right, and Mercury can be seen as a tiny black dot moving across the face of the Sun. This is called a transit. Astronomers watch transits to learn more about Mercury, but they must use special equipment. The Sun's brightness means that it is not safe to look directly at it.

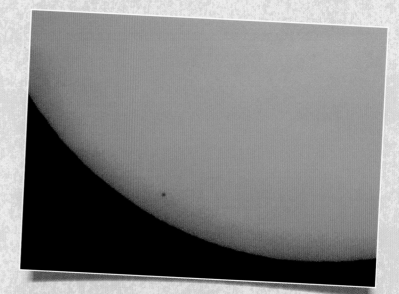

The black dot of Mercury transits across the Sun, highlighting their vast size difference.

FACT FILE

NAME: Mercury	MOONS: 0
SIZE: 4,879 km (3,032 miles) in diameter	

AVERAGE DISTANCE FROM SUN: 58 million km (36 million miles)	LENGTH OF DAY: 58.6 Earth days
	LENGTH OF YEAR: 88 Earth days

VENUS

Venus is the Solar System's second planet, and has an orbit between those of Mercury and Earth. It is a small, rocky planet, similar in size to our own. At some points during the year, it appears just as the Sun sets in the evening, while at others it rises above the horizon in the morning before the Sun. Until the mid-4th century BCE, the ancient Greeks thought it was actually two separate objects – a morning star and an evening star.

The ancient Roman goddess Venus

A BEAUTIFUL NAME

Venus is beautifully bright in the night sky. Like Mercury, it doesn't make its own light – it reflects the light from the Sun. Some ancient peoples named it after female goddesses known for their beauty, such as Ishtar for the Babylonians, Aphrodite for the Greeks, and Venus for the Romans. In the Sanskrit language of ancient India, the planet is called Sukra, meaning 'clear and bright'.

SPOTTING VENUS

Thanks to its nearness to Earth, and to the swirling clouds that reflect sunlight, Venus is the third-brightest object in the sky. In fact, it is so bright that it can sometimes be seen during the day. The best times to see Venus, depending on the time of year, are in the two hours before dawn or after sunset. Late at night, it will have followed the Sun below the horizon and will be out of sight.

Venus at dusk

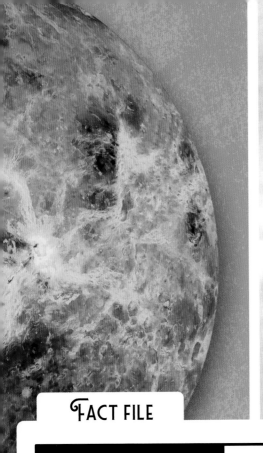

THE UGLY TRUTH

Although Venus is beautiful from a distance, up close it is anything but. Some people call Venus 'Earth's evil twin', because it is nearly the same size, but much less habitable. Venus's thick atmosphere is full of carbon dioxide, and it is surrounded by thick clouds of sulphuric acid. If you could visit Venus, you'd discover that it smells of rotten eggs!

FACT FILE

NAME: Venus	MOONS: 0
SIZE: 24,200 km (15,040 miles) in diameter	
AVERAGE DISTANCE FROM SUN: 108 million km (67 million miles)	
LENGTH OF DAY: 243 Earth days	LENGTH OF YEAR: 223 Earth days

The clouds and gas on Venus as seen from space

LIFE ON VENUS?

Venus's clouds cause a runaway greenhouse effect, trapping the Sun's heat and creating a surface temperature of 475°C (900°F) – hot enough to melt lead. The thick atmosphere means that air pressure is crushingly high. None of the spacecraft that have landed on Venus have been able to last longer than two hours before breaking down. It's unlikely that life forms could exist on the surface, but up in the clouds it's cooler, with less air pressure, and astronomers think there is a possibility that life could exist there.

Several Soviet Venera probes reached the surface of Venus and sent back photos and data, but they only worked for a short time.

The Venusian Surface

Thanks to the thick clouds that block the view, even with a telescope you won't be able to see any of the features on Venus's rocky surface. Everything we know about it comes from spacecraft that have either landed on the planet, or which used radar and other tools to 'see' through the clouds and map it from orbit. The surface is so hot that few craft have landed there.

NASA's Magellan spacecraft sent images of Venus to Earth in the 1990s.

This image of Venus is made up of many pictures captured by Magellan and given false colours to highlight features including valleys and mountains.

Volcanic World

Like our own planet, Venus has an iron core and a mantle (the layer between the core and the outer crust) of hot rock, topped with a thin, rocky crust. On Earth, molten rock from inside the planet erupts onto the surface as volcanoes. The same thing happens on Venus. Over billions of years, these eruptions have shaped the surface. There are valleys and mountains, including many volcanoes. Astronomers have recently discovered evidence that some of the volcanoes may still be active.

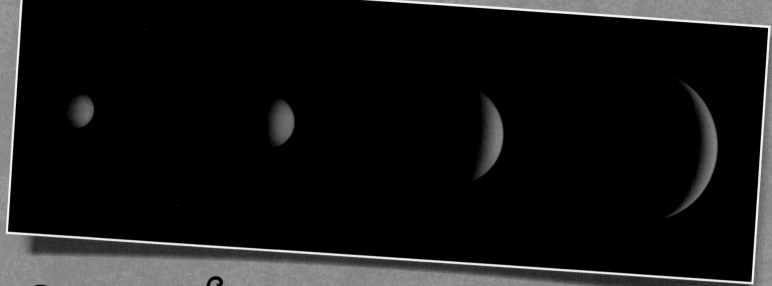

PHASES OF VENUS

If you look at Venus with the naked eye, it's a bright pinprick of light. But if you use binoculars or a small telescope, and observe Venus over a period of several days, you'll notice something amazing – it has phases, just like the Moon (see pages 54–55). It shrinks from a full disc down to a crescent (above), then gradually swells again. But unlike the Moon, which takes 29.5 days to cycle through the phases, Venus takes months to complete its cycle.

OLGA NIKOLAEVA

Many of the features on the surface of Venus are named after goddesses, but certain types of volcanic craters called *paterae* are named after famous women from history. One of Venus's craters (like the one shown right) is named for Olga Nikolaeva, a Russian scientist who spent most of her career studying the surface and atmosphere of Venus. She used her knowledge to help with the design of the Russian robotic landers that sent back data from the surface in the 1970s and 1980s.

BORN: 1941, Russia	DIED: 2000, Russia

GALILEO'S DISCOVERY

The Italian astronomer Galileo (right) discovered Venus's phases back in 1610, using his new telescope (see pages 18–19). This discovery changed our view of the heavens. Most people at the time still believed that Earth was at the centre of the Universe. In 1543, Copernicus (see page 42) had published his theory that the planets actually revolved around the Sun, but many dismissed it as nonsense. Galileo's discovery proved that Copernicus had been right. Venus could only have phases if it orbited the Sun, not Earth. About 30 years later, other astronomers discovered that Mercury has phases too.

MARS

Mars is the fourth planet from the Sun.

It is often called the 'Red Planet' due to its bright reddish colour. In some ways, Mars is similar to our own planet. It has seasons of about the same length as Earth's and features such as mountains, volcanoes and deserts.

SPOTTING Mars

Mars is one of the brightest objects in the night sky, and you can often see its red colour, even with the naked eye. Its brightness makes it fairly easy to find, though you have to know where and when to look. Mars moves around the sky and is not always visible. At its closest point, Mars is only 56 million km (35 million miles) from Earth. This is the best time to get a good look at it. At other times, when it's on the opposite side of the Sun, it is much further away – and harder to see.

Mars often appears very bright in the night sky.

SURFACE FEATURES

Mars is a fairly small, rocky planet, like Earth. There are other similarities, too. With a telescope, you may be able to make out white patches at the planet's top and bottom. These are the polar ice caps (below). Unlike the ice caps on Earth, they are made of a mixture of water ice and frozen carbon dioxide. You may also see light and dark patches on the surface. These are caused by materials that reflect light differently. The surface of Mars has other features, such as craters, canyons and volcanoes, but these are too small to see without a very large telescope.

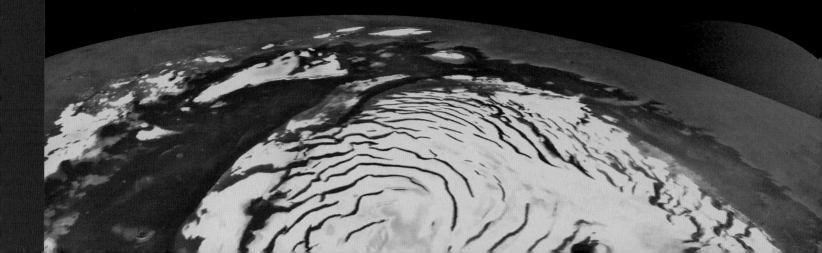

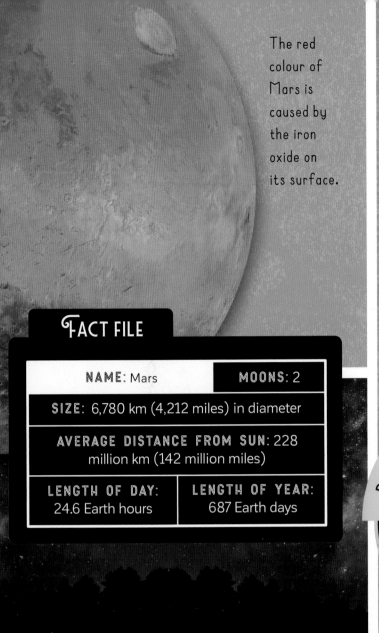

The red colour of Mars is caused by the iron oxide on its surface.

TINY MOONS

Mars has two moons, called Phobos and Deimos. The planet is named after the Roman god of war, and its moons take their names – meaning 'fear' and 'dread' – from the two companions of the Greek god of war. But you won't be able to see them from your back garden! That's because, compared to Earth's moon, they are incredibly tiny. Phobos is the larger of the two, and it is only about 11 km (6 miles) across. Both moons are lumpy, rather than being spherical, and they are covered in craters from space rocks that smashed into them.

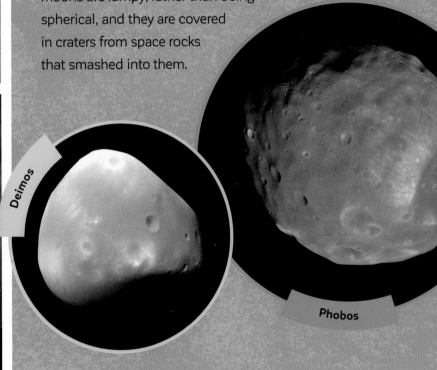

Deimos

Phobos

FACT FILE

NAME: Mars	MOONS: 2
SIZE: 6,780 km (4,212 miles) in diameter	
AVERAGE DISTANCE FROM SUN: 228 million km (142 million miles)	
LENGTH OF DAY: 24.6 Earth hours	LENGTH OF YEAR: 687 Earth days

CANALS ON MARS?

Once astronomers had telescopes big enough to see details on Mars's surface, they began to map it. And they were amazed at what they saw! Giovanni Schiaparelli (1835–1910), an Italian astronomer, saw dark lines that he thought were some sort of channels. On his map, he labelled them as *canali*, the Italian for 'channel'. But others interpreted this as 'canals', believing they had been dug by alien life forms! People wrote books about these 'Martians' and their network of canals, but they turned out to be illusions.

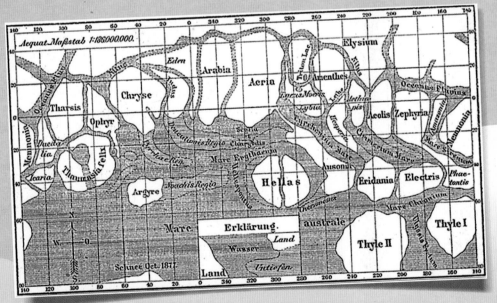

Schiaparelli's drawing of the Martian surface

JUPITER

When it comes to planets, Jupiter is the king. It's absolutely huge – more than twice as massive as all the other planets combined! So it seems fitting that it takes its name from the king of the Roman gods. But in fact, this is a lucky coincidence, because the ancient Romans had no idea that it was the biggest planet when they gave it the name! To the Chinese, it is the 'wood star' – the five planets known about in ancient times were each named after one of the five elements of wood, fire, metal, earth and water.

FACT FILE

NAME: Jupiter	**MOONS:** 79
SIZE: 142,984 km (88,846 miles) in diameter	
AVERAGE DISTANCE FROM SUN: 778 million km (484 million miles)	
LENGTH OF DAY: 9.93 Earth hours	**LENGTH OF YEAR:** 11.86 Earth years

GAS GIANT

Jupiter is very different from the planets closer to Earth. It's not solid and rocky, but made of swirling gas. If you were to take a spacecraft to Jupiter, there would be nowhere to land! The swirling clouds that we see are mainly made of hydrogen and helium, just like the Sun. They give the planet a striped appearance, which you can see with a powerful enough telescope.

The swirling clouds of Jupiter

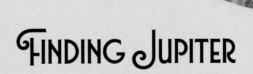

The Great Red Spot on Jupiter

SPINNING AROUND

Like all the planets, Jupiter spins around a central axis. And it spins extremely fast! A day on Jupiter is less than 10 Earth hours long. Because it is so big and made of gas, this fast spinning makes Jupiter bulge out around its equator, just like Earth. It is not round like a ball, but slightly squashed like a football that you've sat on. The surface changes as clouds and storms move and shift. The famous Great Red Spot is a giant storm that has been raging for hundreds of years.

FINDING JUPITER

Although it is a long way from the Sun's light, Jupiter is still a very bright planet. Its clouds reflect the sunlight more than a dark, rocky object would. This means that it's one of the brightest objects in the night sky. Like all the planets, it moves along the ecliptic (see pages 42–43) and appears at different places at different times of year. You'll need to check an app or website to see where to look from your home, but it should be easy to spot.

In 2020, a conjunction of Jupiter (bottom left), Saturn (top left) and the Moon was visible from Earth.

JUPITER'S MOONS

Earth has one moon and Mars has two, but Jupiter has dozens, making it a bit like a mini solar system. Galileo discovered the four largest moons in 1610, and they are called the Galilean moons in his honour. The rest of the moons are much smaller, and it was nearly 300 years before the next one was discovered. You can see the Galilean moons with powerful binoculars or a small telescope. They may not all be visible at once – if a moon is behind or directly in front of Jupiter, you won't see it.

Jupiter and four of its moons captured by the Juno spacecraft in 2016

Io

Io has the most volcanic activity of any body in the Solar System. The planet is caught between the pull of Jupiter's gravity and that of Europa and Ganymede. These powerful forces heat up its inside and fuel its many volcanoes. When they erupt, they shoot out plumes of lava that can be dozens of kilometres high. The constant eruptions give Io a surface that looks a bit like a cosmic pizza.

Volcano

GANYMEDE

Ganymede is the largest moon in the Solar System. In fact, it is larger than Mercury! If it orbited the Sun instead of going around Jupiter, it would be a planet. Ganymede's surface is a mix of dark cratered regions and lighter areas marked with long grooves. The Hubble Space Telescope (see pages 26–27) has recently discovered evidence that Ganymede may have a huge saltwater ocean beneath its icy surface.

CALLISTO

Jupiter's second-largest moon, Callisto, is more cratered than any other body in the Solar System. For a long time, astronomers thought that Callisto was a dead, uninteresting ball of rock and ice, with no volcanoes or tectonic plates. But like Ganymede, Callisto may have a salty subterranean ocean. Callisto's is much deeper, though – probably about 250 km (150 miles) below the surface.

The JUICE probe is being sent to Jupiter's moon Europa to search for life.

EUROPA

Europa has an icy crust about 15–25 km (10–15 miles) thick, surrounding a vast saltwater ocean that probably has about twice the amount of water of Earth's oceans. The crust is marked by long cracks, grooves and ridges. Astronomers think that water from the ocean may occasionally erupt out through the surface in long plumes.

SUBTERRANEAN LIFE?

Europa's ocean made scientists wonder if this little moon might be hiding life. Water, after all, is one of the main requirements for life to exist, as far as we know. Now that it looks as though Ganymede and Callisto have underground oceans too, they are also possible locations for life. A probe called the Jupiter Icy Moons Explorer (JUICE) will look for further clues.

SATURN

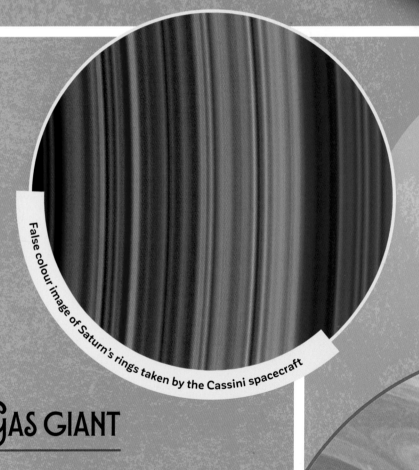

In a line-up of the eight planets, Saturn stands out because of its elegant rings. It's not the only planet to have rings, but Saturn's are the most spectacular. When Galileo looked at Saturn through a telescope in 1610, he saw the rings as bulges on each side, giving the planet an oval shape. He thought they were a pair of moons, one on each side. It wasn't until 1659 that the Dutch astronomer Christiaan Huygens, using a more powerful telescope, realised that they were rings.

WHAT'S IN A NAME?

Easily visible to the naked eye, Saturn was known in ancient times. The Romans named it after their god of agriculture and wealth. In Hindu mythology, the planet was known as Shani, after a god who delivers justice based on whether a person did good deeds in their life. To the ancient Chinese, it was the earth star. Saturday is named after Saturn, and in the Hebrew language spoken in Israel, Saturn is called Shabbatai, meaning 'the Sabbath planet'. For Jewish people, Saturday is the weekly holy day, known as the Sabbath.

False colour image of Saturn's rings taken by the Cassini spacecraft

GAS GIANT

Saturn is very similar to Jupiter, its nearest planetary neighbour. It is a giant ball of hydrogen and helium that spins very fast – a day on Saturn is just under 11 hours long. Below the layers of swirling clouds, there is a layer of liquid hydrogen. Saturn may have a solid core of metal and rock, but it is still not very dense. In fact, if you could put it in a bathtub large enough, Saturn would float!

NAME: Saturn	MOONS: 82
SIZE: 116,464 km (72,366 miles) in diameter	
AVERAGE DISTANCE FROM SUN: 1.4 billion km (886 million miles)	
LENGTH OF DAY: 10.7 Earth hours	LENGTH OF YEAR: 29 Earth years

STRIPED PLANET

Saturn's clouds give it a striped appearance that you may be able to see faintly through a small telescope. The clouds form bands of yellow, tan and orange. Saturn looks peaceful and serene, but these clouds are actually moved around by incredibly strong winds. In some places they blow at speeds of 500 metres (1,600 ft) per second – more than four times as fast as the strongest hurricane winds on Earth.

The swirling clouds of Saturn

GIAN DOMENICO CASSINI

Born in Italy, astronomer Gian Domenico Cassini spent a large part of his career in France, working for King Louis XIV. He discovered four moons of Saturn, as well as a gap in the rings that is now named after him (see pages 72–73). In 1997, NASA launched a spacecraft called Cassini to explore Saturn and its moons. It spent 13 years orbiting Saturn, sending back a huge amount of information.

	BORN: 1625, Perinaldo, Republic of Genoa
	DIED: 1712, Paris, France

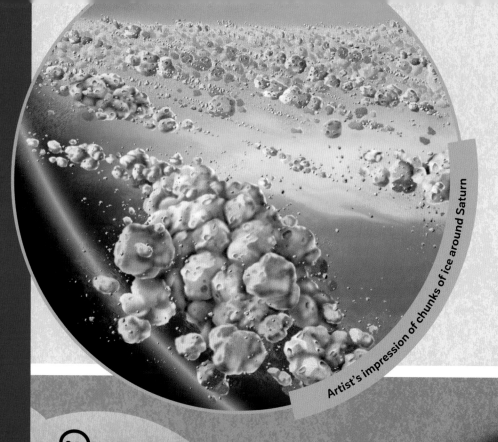

Artist's impression of chunks of ice around Saturn

SATURN'S RINGS

Saturn's rings spread out in a flat plane extending from the planet's equator, like the brim of a hat. They are made up of billions of small chunks of rock and ice. Some pieces are no bigger than a speck of dust, while others are as big as a house, or even larger. They are probably fragments of a small moon smashed apart by a comet millions of years ago (probably between 10 and 100 million years ago).

BY THE NUMBERS

The rings stretch out about 232,000 km (175,000 miles) from Saturn, but they are extremely flat, with an average vertical height of only about 10 metres (33 ft). The rings were given letters in the order they were discovered, so these letters don't match up with their positions. The closest ring to Saturn is the dusty D ring, followed by the C ring and the B ring. Then there is a large gap called the Cassini Division (see page 71) before you reach the A, F, G and E rings.

D

Cassini Division

B

Saturn's rings backlit by the Sun, allowing them to be seen in detail

DISAPPEARING RINGS

With an amateur telescope, you'll probably only be able to make out the three largest rings (A, B and C). But sometimes you won't see anything! This is because Saturn tilts on its axis, like Earth does. This tilt gives Saturn seasons, and it also means that at some points in its orbit, the plane of the rings is directly in line with the Sun, making them hard to see.

Saturn's largest moon, Titan, seen here alongside the planet's rings

Many Moons

Saturn currently has as many known moons as Jupiter, and there could well be more to be discovered. The largest moon, Titan, is bigger than Mercury, while the smallest ones are roughly the size of a large football stadium. Some of the smaller moons orbit within the rings, and in fact, the objects that make up the rings could also be considered to be tiny moons, because they orbit the planet.

F

C   A   G   E

Terrific Titan

For a moon, Titan is a whopper. It's also incredibly interesting! It's the only moon in the Solar System that we know has a substantial atmosphere. It's also the only place other than Earth that has liquid rivers, lakes and seas on its surface. But Titan's clouds and lakes aren't made of water – they are mainly liquid methane. Methane is usually a gas on Earth but Titan is so cold that it becomes a liquid. Scientists think that Titan may be home to some form of life.

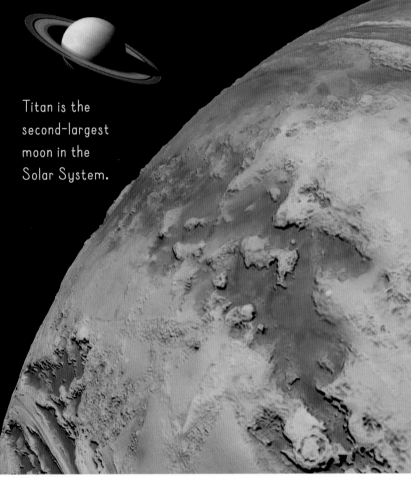

Titan is the second-largest moon in the Solar System.

Plumes of ice erupt from the surface of Enceladus

Weird and Wonderful

Saturn's other moons are also interesting. Hyperion is potato-shaped, with a weird cratered surface giving it a sponge-like appearance. Mimas has a huge crater that makes it a dead ringer for the Death Star. Pan and Atlas have ridges around their equator, giving them a flying saucer appearance. One half of Iapetus is black, while the other half is white, and the icy moon Enceladus probably has an ocean under the ice and has as good a chance of having life as Europa.

ICE GIANTS

Jupiter and Saturn are called gas giants because they are huge and made of gas. It's pretty logical. The next two planets, Uranus and Neptune, are ice giants. While the gas giants are mainly made up of hydrogen and helium, the ice giants have other elements including oxygen and carbon. They have big cores that are icy and rocky, surrounded by slushy water and ammonia ice. Only the very outer shells are gas.

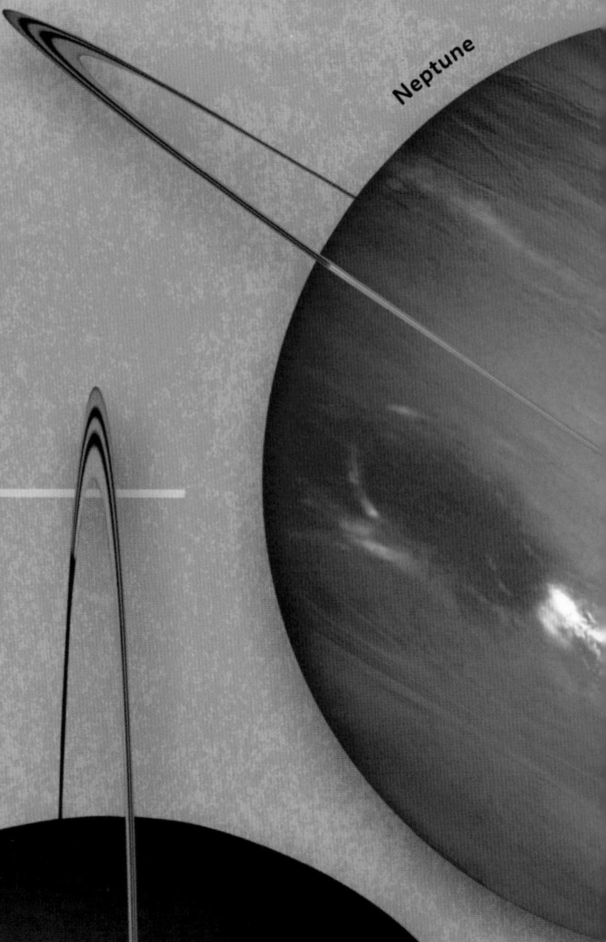

TWIN PLANETS?

Uranus and Neptune have a lot in common. They are nearly the same size (Uranus is slightly wider, but Neptune has more mass). They are a similar colour, with Uranus a beautiful pale turquoise and Neptune a deeper blue. They both rotate very fast, and their distance from the Sun makes them incredibly cold. Both have a collection of moons and a system of rings.

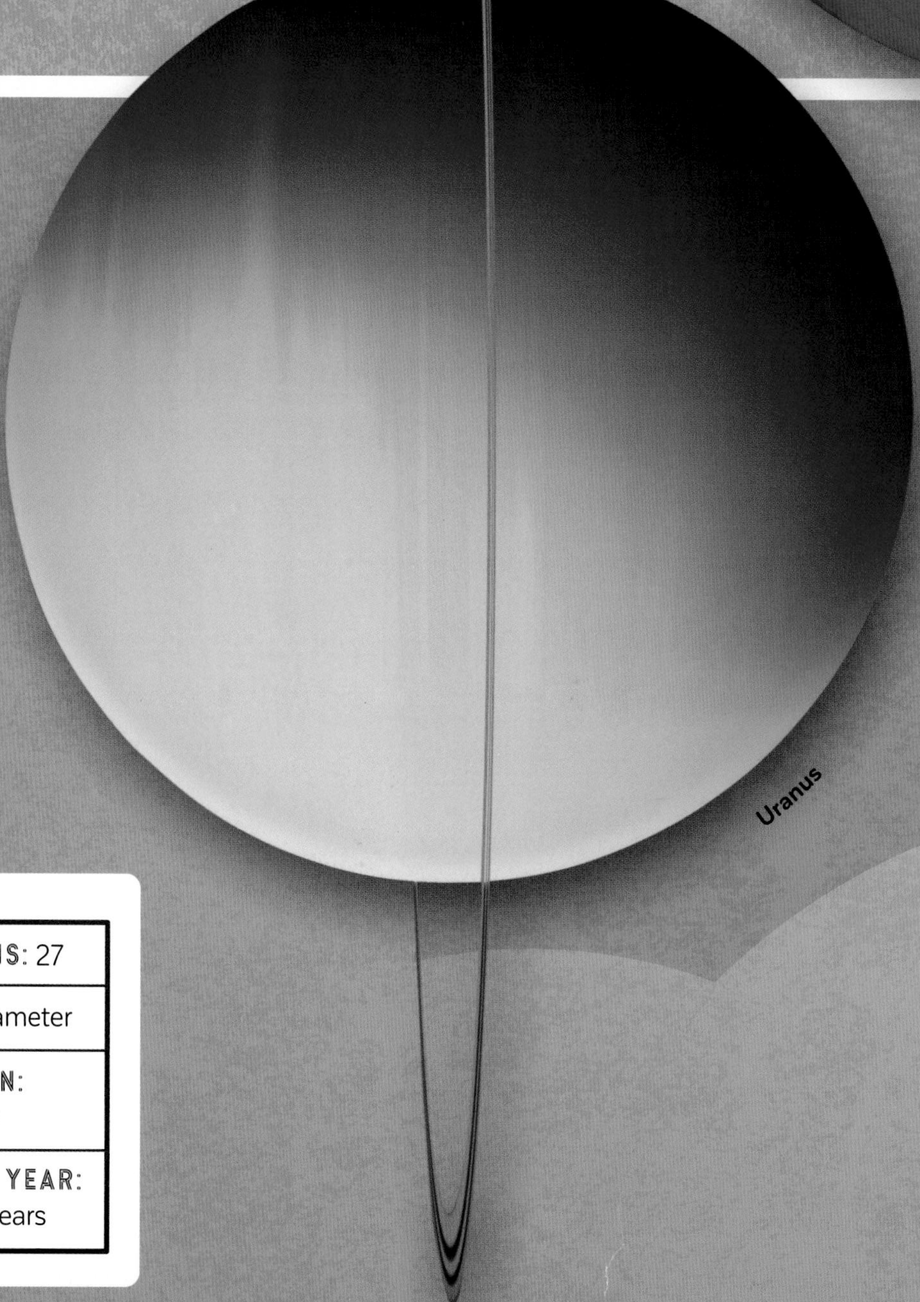

Neptune

Uranus

FACT FILE

NAME: Uranus	MOONS: 27
SIZE: 50,724 km (31,518 miles) in diameter	
AVERAGE DISTANCE FROM SUN: 2.9 billion km (1.8 billion miles)	
LENGTH OF DAY: 17.25 Earth hours	**LENGTH OF YEAR:** 84 Earth years

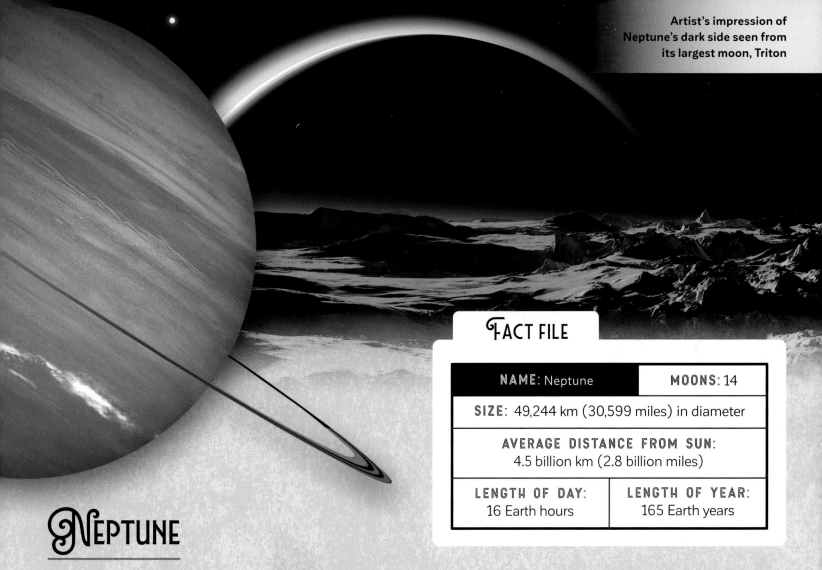

FACT FILE

NAME: Neptune	MOONS: 14
SIZE: 49,244 km (30,599 miles) in diameter	
AVERAGE DISTANCE FROM SUN: 4.5 billion km (2.8 billion miles)	
LENGTH OF DAY: 16 Earth hours	LENGTH OF YEAR: 165 Earth years

Neptune

Neptune is too small and far away to see without a telescope. With binoculars, it looks like a star, but with a telescope you may be able to see a disc shape, and the blue colour should be obvious. In fact, Neptune is so far away that it takes 165 years to travel around the Sun. It takes over four hours for light to reach Earth from Neptune. From the surface of Neptune, the Sun would look like a very bright star, and midday would feel like a dim twilight.

Unusual Uranus

Despite the similarities with Neptune, Uranus is unique. Its axis is tilted more than 90 degrees, which means that it rotates more or less on its side. The rings and moons follow this tilt too. It means that for part of Uranus's orbit, the Sun shines directly on the north pole, leaving the southern hemisphere in complete darkness for 21 Earth years! On the other side of its orbit, the seasons are reversed. You can see Uranus with the naked eye if it's very dark and you know where to look. With a decent telescope, you may be able to see a tiny blue-green disc shape.

Clouds and Storms

One thing that the gas giants and the ice giants have in common is storms. Their clouds are swept along by giant storms with high winds. This means that the planets' surfaces often change their appearance, though you'll need a powerful telescope to see them. A region of bright clouds can indicate a storm, and dark spots sometimes appear too. Astronomers use powerful telescopes like Hubble (see pages 26–27) and the Keck Observatory in Hawaii to study these planets.

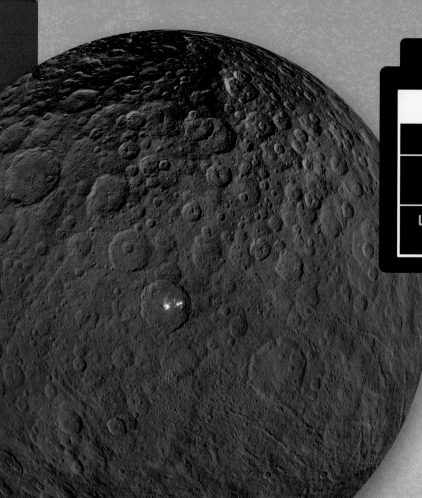

Ceres

Pluto

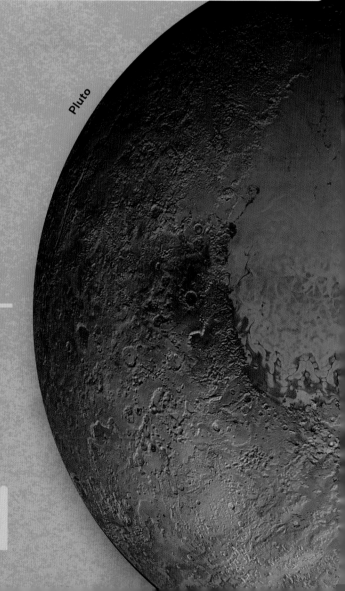

DWARF PLANETS

For 76 years, Neptune was not the last planet in the Solar System. It was the eighth of nine, with small, rocky Pluto orbiting (mostly) beyond it. But by the early 2000s, astronomers had a problem. Pluto was part of a ring of icy objects called the Kuiper Belt. More and more objects were being discovered there, some of them similar in size. If Pluto was a planet, were these other objects planets too? How many planets did our Solar System have?

DOWNGRADES AND UPGRADES

In 2006, astronomers agreed on a controversial new definition of planets. These are objects that orbit the Sun and are big enough for their gravity to pull themselves into a rounded shape. They must also be massive enough to clear the area around them of smaller objects. Pluto meets the first two requirements, but not the third. It was therefore downgraded to a new category: dwarf planet. At the same time, an asteroid called Ceres was upgraded to a dwarf planet. So far, there are three other official dwarf planets: Eris, Haumea and Makemake. All three are far beyond the orbit of Neptune.

Artist's impression of the dwarf planet Eris and its moon Dysnomia

CERES

When Ceres was upgraded in 2006, it wasn't the first time this object had been reclassified. The Italian astronomer Giuseppe Piazzi was the first person to spot it, in 1801. At first, he thought it was a comet, before changing his mind and deciding it was a planet. In 1863, astronomers decided to call it an asteroid. Unlike the other dwarf planets discovered so far, the orbit of Ceres is between Mars and Jupiter. It is small (much smaller than Pluto) and rocky, but its mantle may be made of frozen water.

EXPLORING PLUTO

Pluto is so small and far away that, for many years, the only photographs we had of it were fuzzy blobs (only advanced amateur astronomers will be able to spot it). That all changed in 2015 when the New Horizons spacecraft flew past Pluto. It sent back amazing images and loads of data, showing that Pluto's surface had tall mountains and deep valleys, as well as giant ice sheets made of frozen nitrogen. There may be a liquid ocean beneath the surface, sending out cold, slushy liquid water through strange volcano-like structures.

ASTEROIDS

Ceres has a lot of neighbours in its part of the Solar System. Millions of small rocky objects form a belt, orbiting the Sun between Mars and Jupiter. These asteroids can be up to hundreds of kilometres in diameter. They are leftovers from the creation of our Solar System. And despite what sci-fi films show, they are not tightly packed – the average distance between two asteroids is about a million kilometres!

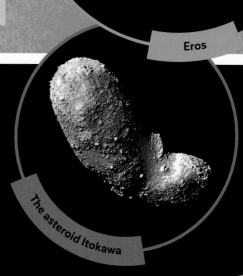

Eros

The asteroid Itokawa

THE CELESTIAL POLICE

In the late 1700s, astronomers became convinced that there was another planet, somewhere between the orbits of Mars and Jupiter. A group of astronomers teamed up to find the missing planet, calling themselves the Celestial Police. They didn't find it (because it doesn't exist!), but they did find some of the first asteroids, including Pallas, Juno and Vesta.

Vesta

FACT FILE

NAME: Vesta	MOONS: 0	LENGTH OF DAY: 5.34 Earth hours
SIZE: 530 km (329 miles) in diameter		
AVERAGE DISTANCE FROM SUN: 353 million km (219 million miles)		LENGTH OF YEAR: 1325 Earth days

Two members of the Celestial Police

Franz Von Zach

Heinrich Olbers

ROCKY WORLDS

Ida

Asteroids are mainly rock, metal or a mix of the two. Only the biggest ones are round(ish), and most are lumpy and irregularly shaped. Many asteroids are covered in impact craters. They tumble around as they orbit the Sun. In 1994, astronomers discovered that the asteroid Ida has a tiny moon, called Dactyl. Since then, more than 150 asteroids have been found with one or more moons.

Dactyl

The asteroid Ida and its tiny moon Dactyl

SPOTTING ASTEROIDS

Although the asteroid belt is relatively close to Earth, asteroids' small size makes them difficult to spot. You need clear skies and a telescope, and even then, it's hard to tell them from stars. The best way is to draw a chart of the stars surrounding the object you think is an asteroid, then look again a few nights later. If the object has moved relative to the stars, it's probably an asteroid.

OTHER ASTEROIDS

Although the majority of asteroids are located in the asteroid belt, some of them get kicked out by the force of Jupiter's gravity, and a few of these end up crossing the orbits of other planets – including Earth. There are also asteroids called trojans that share another planet's orbit. There are many trojans near Jupiter, and astronomers have also discovered trojans near Mars and Neptune, as well as at least one near Earth.

Space probe Lucy set off in 2021 to explore the asteroid belt.

COMETS

Stars, planets and asteroids are pretty reliable – apart from some seasonal differences, they are always there. But comets are different. These icy bodies swoop in from the furthest edges of the Solar System. With its long tail sweeping behind it, a comet may brighten the sky for a few days, or even several months. Then it disappears, returning back to where it came from. It may come back in a few years, a few centuries, or not at all.

Coma

Nucleus

The spectacular
Comet McNaught,
seen in 2007

WARNINGS FROM THE SKIES

The word 'disaster' derives from the Latin words for 'bad star', and many ancient cultures feared comets. They saw them as bad omens – signs that something terrible was going to happen. Comets were spectacular yet unpredictable, so they must be messages from the gods, right? But sometimes comets were seen as a sign that a great person had been born. The star that the Magi followed to Bethlehem after the birth of Jesus may have actually been a comet. A comet also appeared after the murder of the Roman ruler Julius Caesar. His successor claimed this was a sign that Caesar had turned into a god.

Halley's Comet was viewed as an evil omen on the Bayeux Tapestry, which dates from the 11th century.

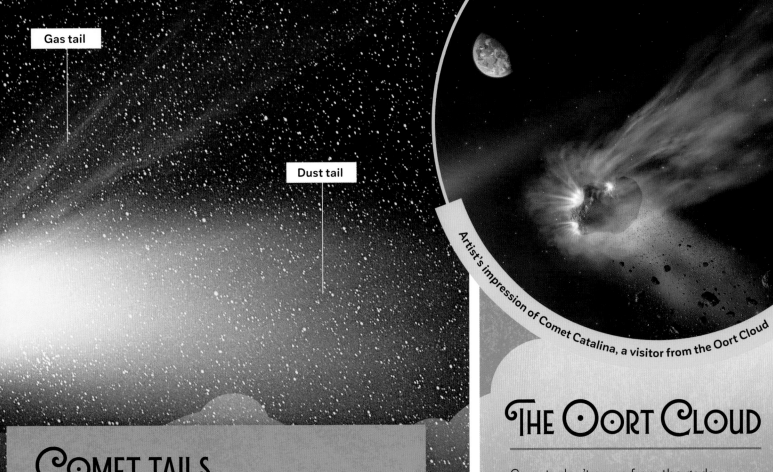

Gas tail

Dust tail

Artist's impression of Comet Catalina, a visitor from the Oort Cloud

Comet Tails

Comets are often called 'dirty snowballs' because they are made of ice and dust. As a comet approaches the Sun, its body – called the nucleus – begins to get warmer. The ice starts to turn into gas, forming a cloud called a coma around the nucleus. The comet forms two tails, one of gas, one of dust. Thanks to the pushing force of something called the solar wind, a comet's tail always points away from the Sun, even if that means the tail is travelling ahead of the nucleus.

The Oort Cloud

Comets don't come from the gods, regardless of what the Romans thought. Like asteroids, comets are leftover bits from the days when the Solar System first formed. But unlike asteroids, which are rocky and metallic, comets are icy. Some come from the Kuiper Belt, while others come from the distant Oort Cloud (see page 59), which lies beyond it. Because it is so far away, we still know very little about the Oort Cloud.

A Comet's Journey

Comets travel in a long, looping path around the Sun (see right). Those that take less than 200 years to complete an orbit are called short-period comets, and they mainly come from the Kuiper Belt. Long-period comets, which come from the Oort Cloud, can take up to 30 million years to complete a trip! From Earth, we can only see comets when they get to the inner Solar System. Some comets are faint and hard to see, while others shine brightly across the sky for weeks on end.

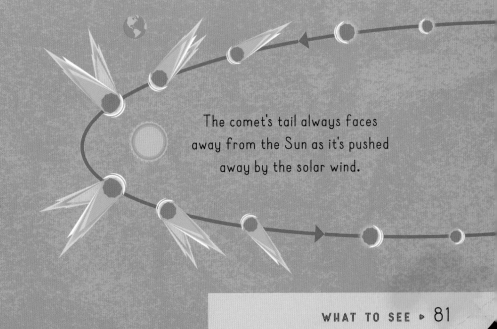

The comet's tail always faces away from the Sun as it's pushed away by the solar wind.

METEORS

Have you ever made a wish on a shooting star streaking across the sky? Despite the name, these mini-fireballs are not stars at all. In fact, they're much, much closer to you than the stars are! They are meteors – small rocks that burn up as they hurtle through Earth's atmosphere. Spotting a meteor is pure luck, as there is no way to predict when or where they will appear. However, they can be seen with greater frequency during a meteor shower.

Big meteors can look like fireballs in the sky.

SPACE ROCKS

Meteoroids are rocks in space, ranging from tiny grains to small asteroids. They are often pieces of other objects – such as comets, asteroids, planets or moons – that have been blasted off by an impact. They tumble through space, and some of them end up approaching Earth. As they fall through Earth's atmosphere, friction makes them heat up and glow.

SMALL BUT BRIGHT

Very rarely, a large meteoroid will cause a huge fireball in the sky, like the one that lit up Chelyabinsk, Russia, in 2013. But the majority of meteoroids that enter our atmosphere are no bigger than a small pebble. You'd never be able to see an object this size if it were miles away, so how can we see meteors? It's all down to their speed. When a meteoroid enters Earth's atmosphere, it is often travelling at up to 72 km (45 miles) per second. The friction this creates heats up the rock to very high temperatures, and releases energy that we see as light.

The trail left in the sky after the 2013 meteor seen over Russia

WHAT'S IN A NAME?

A meteor goes by different names depending on where it is. A rock in space that could become a meteor is called a meteoroid. When it is burning up in Earth's atmosphere, it is a meteor. And if part of the rock survives re-entry and lands on Earth, it is called a meteorite. These rocks (right) are very valuable to scientists because they are pieces of other worlds.

This crater in Australia was made when a meteorite hit Earth about 120,000 years ago.

METEOR SHOWERS

There are usually several meteors per hour, but during a meteor shower those numbers go up. These are times of the year when Earth passes through the trail of debris left behind by a comet. These showers happen at the same time each year, and they are named after the constellation where the meteors seem to originate. So the Orionids seem to come from the constellation of Orion, and the meteors are caused by debris left by Halley's Comet, which last passed into the inner Solar System in 1986. In mid-December, the Geminids put on one of the best shows with about 120 meteors per hour at the peak.

A time-lapse photo of the Perseid meteor shower, which takes place between July and August each year

ARTIFICIAL OBJECTS

Sputnik 1, the first satellite, was launched in 1957.

Most of the objects in the Solar System are natural, having formed billions of years ago. But a few of the things we can see in space are much, much newer. In fact, it's humans that put them there! In the decades since 1957, when the first artificial satellite was launched into orbit, thousands of satellites have been sent up. They provide GPS service, beam communication signals, track weather systems, and more.

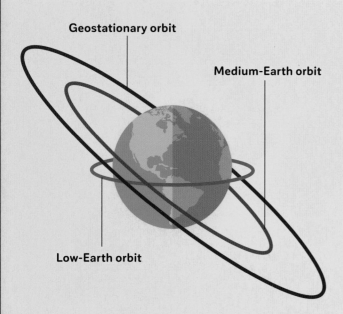

Geostationary orbit

Medium-Earth orbit

Low-Earth orbit

HOW HIGH?

A large proportion of satellites are in low-Earth orbit, just a few hundred kilometres above Earth. These include the International Space Station and the Hubble Space Telescope. A small fraction are in medium-Earth orbit, around 20,000 km (12,500 miles) high. The satellites that are even higher, at 35,785 km (22,236 miles), are in what's called geostationary orbit. The speed of their orbit matches the speed of Earth's rotation, so they stay above the same point all the time.

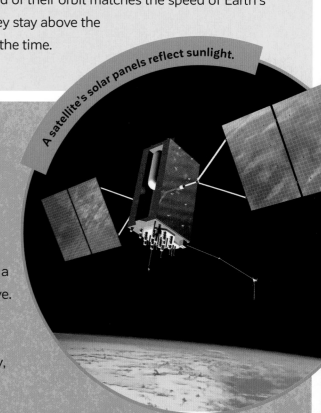

A satellite's solar panels reflect sunlight.

METEOR OR SATELLITE?

On a clear night, you can see satellites in the sky, especially those that are in low-Earth orbit. They reflect light from the Sun (their solar panels are especially good for reflecting), so they are best spotted in the hours just after sunset or before sunrise. A satellite will appear as a small point of light, like a star, but the difference is that satellites move. Choose a section of sky and watch to see if anything moves. If it has blinking lights, it's an aeroplane, and if it moves quickly for a short distance and then disappears, it's a meteor. A satellite moves steadily, in a straight line, taking a few minutes to travel across the entire sky.

THE INTERNATIONAL SPACE STATION

The International Space Station (ISS), below, is an orbiting laboratory where astronauts from different countries live and work. As the largest human-made object in space, it is also the easiest to spot. It can appear as bright as Venus or Jupiter to viewers on Earth, and sometimes has a yellow tinge as its solar panels reflect the Sun. The ISS orbits Earth 16 times a day – once every 90 minutes – but it is not visible from all parts of Earth on each pass. There are apps and websites that can tell you where and when to look. On each pass it will be visible for a few minutes, as it rises above the horizon, moves across the sky, and then dips below the horizon again.

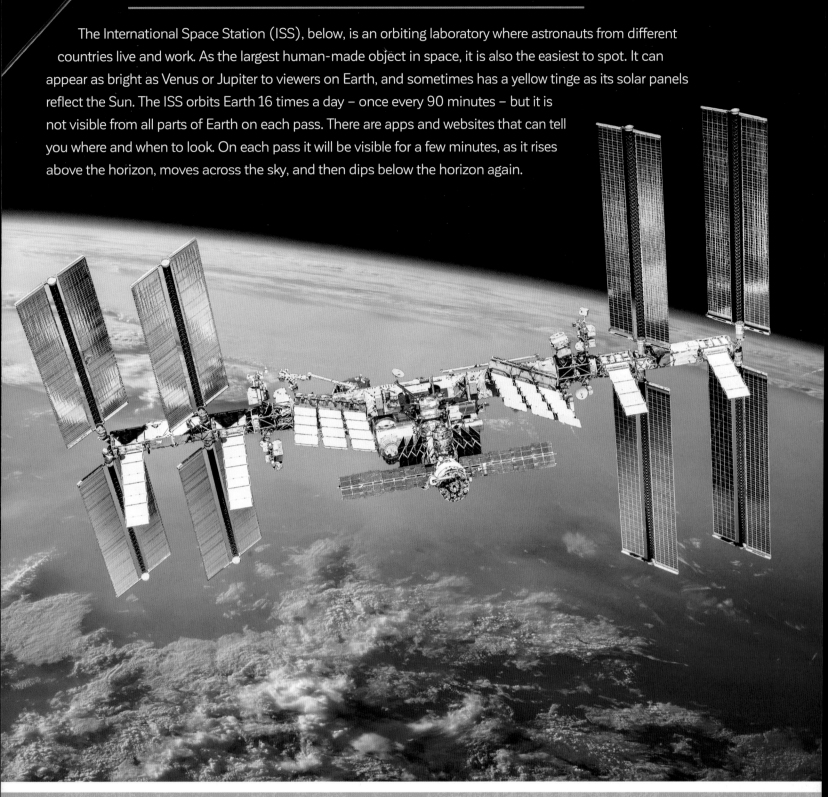

BUILDING A SPACE STATION

At roughly the size of a football pitch, the ISS was much too big to launch into orbit all at once. Instead, it was built in modules that were launched and then assembled once in orbit around Earth. The first two modules, the Russian Zarya and the American Unity, were launched in 1998 and connected in orbit. More pieces were added over the years, and astronauts have been living and working there since 2000.

STARS AND GALAXIES

On a clear, dark night you can often see a river of light stretching across the sky. This amazing sight is a band of billions of stars called the Milky Way – our home galaxy! All of the stars you see in the sky are part of the Milky Way. But it is just one of billions of galaxies that make up the Universe.

The stunning Whirlpool Galaxy is a spiral galaxy 31 million light years from Earth.

WHAT IS A GALAXY?

A galaxy is a system of stars, dust and gas held together by gravitational forces. Many galaxies have a black hole at the centre. Scientists think that there are more than 200 billion galaxies in the Universe. Galaxies are divided into three main types according to their shape: elliptical, spiral and irregular.

The Andromeda Galaxy is an example of a barred spiral galaxy.

The Small Magellanic Cloud is a dwarf irregular galaxy.

Our Home Galaxy

Long ago, before electricity lit up our towns and cities, the skies were much darker. As long as the Moon wasn't too bright, it would have been easy to see the sweep of the Milky Way every clear night. Myths and legends are often an attempt to explain the natural world, so it's no surprise that there is a huge range of legends about this river of light in the sky.

The hazy clouds of the Milky Way are made up of stars, dust and gas.

Milky Way Stories

To the Hungarian people, the Milky Way is the 'road of warriors'. According to legend, if the Hungarians are ever threatened, Prince Csaba (left) – the mythical son of the fierce warrior leader Attila the Hun – will gallop down this pathway to help them. The stars are sparks cast by the shoes of his soldiers' horses. To the Greeks, the Milky Way was actual milk, produced by the goddess Hera to feed the legendary hero Heracles as a baby.

A Galactic Love Story

Chinese legends tell of a cowherd, Niulang, who fell in love with a fairy called Zhinu. They married and had children, but the Goddess of Heaven – angry that a fairy had married a mortal – demanded that Zhinu be brought back to heaven. She slashed her hairpin across the sky, creating a river (the Milky Way) that would keep Niulang from coming to rescue his wife. But the magpies felt sorry for the lovers, and once a year they flock together, forming a bridge across the Milky Way so that Niulang and Zhinu (represented by the stars Altair and Vega) can be reunited.

Niulang and Zhinu

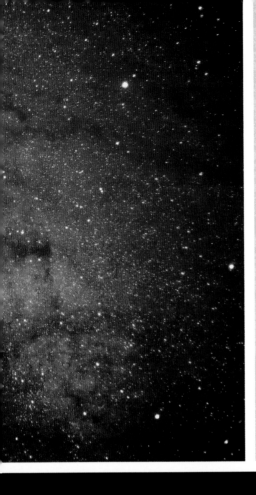

NAMING THE GALAXY

The Milky Way has different names in different languages, and many of them are linked to the myths that people tell. Some are local translations of the same basic idea, such as 'milky road', 'silver river', 'straw path' or even 'bird's path' (because some peoples in northern Europe noticed that migrating birds followed the course of the Milky Way). The modern word 'galaxy' comes from the Greek name for the Milky Way: *galaxias kyklos*, meaning 'milky circle'. So, when we talk about galaxies, we're literally calling them 'milkies'!

Migrating birds

THE COLD HARD FACTS

Of course, the Milky Way isn't actually milk, or straw, or a river, or anything like that. It's our home galaxy, and it appears as a line because we're looking at the galaxy's disc edge-on. Astronomers have recently discovered that the Milky Way is not actually flat; it's more of a flattened S-shape. Our Solar System sits in an arm called the Orion Arm, which is about 27,000 light years from the centre of the galaxy.

Orion Arm

WHAT ARE STARS?

To some ancient people, the stars were gods, or the spirits of people who had died. They watched them move through the sky, but they had no idea of what stars were actually like. Some thought they were balls of fire, but no one knew that the twinkling lights in the night sky were the same type of object as the Sun that lit the day.

Artist's impression of the energy inside a star

⊙NE AND THE SAME

The idea that stars are like the Sun was suggested thousands of years ago by the ancient Greek astronomers Anaxagoras and Aristarchus, but no one took much notice. In the 1500s, the Italian philosopher Giordano Bruno proposed the same thing, but took it a step further, suggesting that distant stars might be surrounded by planets that possibly had life on them. It still took some time for this idea to catch on, and will take even longer for it to be proved.

Giordano Bruno (1548-1600) had controversial theories about the Universe.

INSIDE A STAR

Stars are giant balls of hydrogen and helium, but although they look fiery, they are not actually burning. Deep inside, in a star's core, a nuclear reaction is taking place. The heat and pressure in the core are so great that hydrogen atoms fuse together to form helium atoms. This process releases a huge amount of energy, and some of it reaches us as light and heat. The fusion energy makes the star expand, while the gravity of its immense mass makes it contract. As long as these two forces are balanced, the star will shine brightly.

HOW STARS FORM

Stars first form from clouds of gas and dust, called nebulas. These clouds swirl around, creating little knots of mass. All objects with mass have gravity, so the pull of this gravity attracts more gas and dust, and the cloud begins to collapse inwards. This makes the material at the centre heat up to form a protostar. The bigger it gets, the greater the pull of its gravity, and the more material it can attract. Once it is big enough, the centre becomes hot enough and nuclear fusion will begin.

NAMING STARS

In medieval times, astronomers in the Islamic world kept careful records of stars, and many of the names they gave them are still used today. Bright stars like Deneb, Altair, Betelgeuse and Aldebaran all have Arabic names. Many other stars have Greek names. In 2019, the International Astronomical Union (IAU) – the group that oversees official names for space objects – celebrated the Year of Indigenous Languages. They gave countries around the world the right to use indigenous languages to name one of 112 stars, as well as the planets that orbit it.

Artist's impression of Betelgeuse (see page 117)

This image, captured by NASA's Spitzer Space Telescope, shows thousands of young stars in the Orion Nebula (see pages 140–141).

Same, but different

From Earth, distant stars all look similar. Some are brighter than others, but if you look more closely, you might see that some of them have slightly different colours. Using powerful telescopes and special scientific tools, astronomers have discovered that they also vary in size and are made up of different proportions of elements.

The spiral galaxy NGC 613 contains billions of stars.

Main Sequence

Once a protostar forms inside a nebula, it stays that way for about 100,000 years. Gravity makes it collapse and heat up, and it eventually becomes something called a T Tauri star, which appears bright because of its gravitational energy – but there is no nuclear fusion taking place yet. It stays this way for about 100 million years. Then it becomes what is called a main sequence star, producing energy through fusion. The majority of stars in the Universe are main sequence stars, but they vary in size, colour and brightness.

BIG AND SMALL

The minimum size for a star is about 0.08 times the mass of our Sun. Although this seems like a fairly small object, it's still 80 times the mass of Jupiter. Any smaller than that, and nuclear fusion can't take place. The biggest stars may have 100 times the mass of the Sun. Not surprisingly, the biggest stars tend to be the hottest and the brightest. They have a blue colour, and they burn through their fuel relatively quickly (lasting millions of years). Smaller stars are dimmer and cooler, with a yellow, orange or red colour. The smallest stars may end up burning for trillions of years.

Artist's impression of a blue supergiant star

ANNIE JUMP CANNON

Annie Jump Cannon was an astronomer who worked as a 'human computer' at the Harvard Observatory. Cannon, and women like her, did the painstaking work of recording and classifying stars, performing complicated calculations. She developed a system of classifying stars based on their spectra (see below), which turned out to be linked to their temperature. Using this system, which is still used today, Cannon published a catalogue of 1,122 stars in 1901.

BORN:
1863, Dover, Delaware

DIED:
1941, Cambridge, Massachusetts

STAR SPECTRA

Astronomers in the 1800s used spectrographs (see page 22) to study stars. They seemed to show that different stars were made up of different chemical elements, though it turns out that the real reason the spectra were different is that the stars were different temperatures. But using the star's spectra still allowed astronomers to classify them into groups (see below). The system includes seven types: O, B, A, F, G, K and M. O stars are the biggest, brightest and hottest. M stars are small, dim and cool. The Sun is a G-class star called a yellow dwarf.

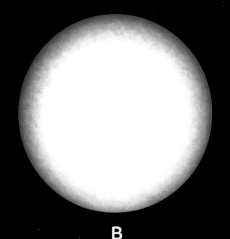

B

A

F

G

K

M

CONSTELLATIONS

Humans have a natural inclination to look for patterns in everything, including the natural world. It's a way of learning and making decision-making easier. Our brains have evolved to see patterns and pictures, such as faces, in nature, even if the 'pattern' turns out to be just a coincidence. So it's no surprise that for thousands of years, humans have organised the random sprinkling of stars in the sky into pictures and shapes.

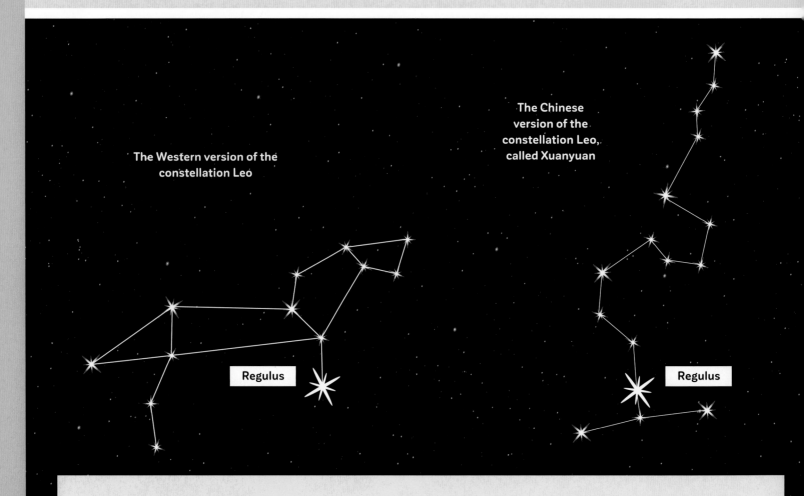

The Western version of the constellation Leo

Regulus

The Chinese version of the constellation Leo, called Xuanyuan

Regulus

PICTURES IN THE SKY

Not everyone who looks at the sky sees the same thing. In fact, different cultures have come up with different groupings of stars, and even when the groups are the same, they often represent different things. Take the constellation Leo, which represents a lion (see page 100). This is what Egyptian stargazers saw, and Arabic astronomers too. The bright star Regulus represented the lion's heart. But Chinese astronomers chose a different selection of stars near Regulus. Connecting them makes a completely different shape, which represented a deity called Xuanyuan (the Yellow Emperor). For people on the Italian island of Sardinia, Regulus and the nearby stars formed a sickle.

NEAR AND FAR

The stars in a constellation are close to each other in the sky, but that doesn't mean that they're actually close to each other in real space. The patterns that appear to viewers on Earth are completely different to what you would see from a different point in the Milky Way. The stars in a constellation can be many, many light years apart. For example, in Orion (see pages 116–117), the shoulder star known as Bellatrix is about 200 light years from Earth, but Mintaka – one of the stars in the belt – is 1,200 light years away!

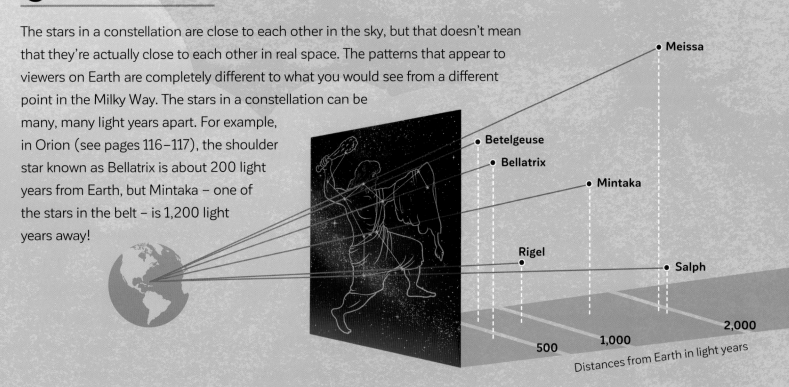

- Meissa
- Betelgeuse
- Bellatrix
- Mintaka
- Rigel
- Salph

500   1,000   2,000

Distances from Earth in light years

STAR NAMES

The International Astronomical Union (IAU) is group of scientists responsible for making sure that stars have a consistent naming system. Most stars are named after the constellation they are part of. They're given letters using the Greek alphabet, with 'alpha' (the first letter) usually being assigned to the brightest star in the constellation. The second-brightest star is 'beta', the third is 'gamma', and so on. Using this system, the brightest star in the constellation of Cygnus (see page 112) is officially Alpha Cygni. However, many people still know it as Deneb, the name by which it has been known for many centuries. The star Albireo, which has the official name Beta Cygni, is less bright.

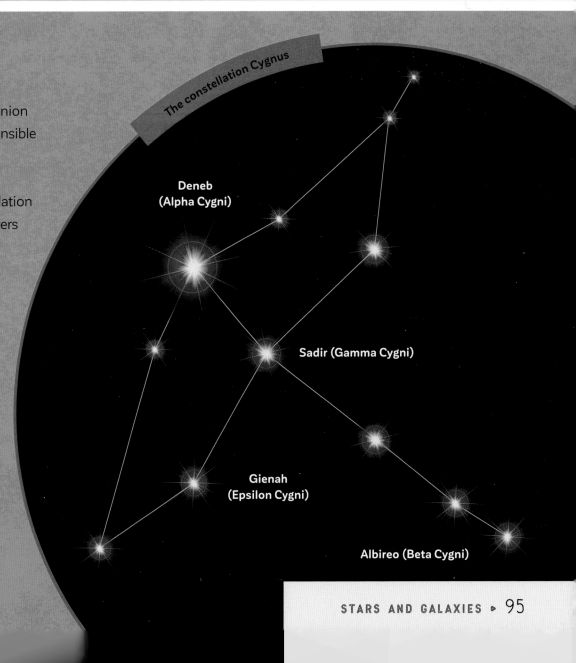

The constellation Cygnus

Deneb (Alpha Cygni)

Sadir (Gamma Cygni)

Gienah (Epsilon Cygni)

Albireo (Beta Cygni)

⊙RGANISING THE SKY

With so many different interpretations of the stars, how can people around the world agree on what they're looking at? The solution was to make a system that everyone followed. So, the IAU stepped up, and in the 1920s they agreed a list of 88 'official' constellations. Stargazers from different cultures continue to look for their own familiar shapes, but having an official list means that astronomers are all on the same page.

Each constellation represents a region of space. The regions fit together like jigsaw pieces.

A GIANT JIGSAW

Remember the old idea that the stars were fixed to a celestial sphere (see pages 40–43)? Well, imagine that the sphere actually is a 3D jigsaw puzzle. There are 88 pieces, each a different shape, but they fit together to make a perfect sphere. If you could shrink yourself down and place yourself at the exact centre of it, you could look up and see an accurate map of the sky. Each piece is not just a group of stars that make a picture – it's a clearly defined section of the sky and all the stars within it, whether they form part of the shape or not.

ANCIENT ORIGINS

Many of the 88 official constellations still have the names and shapes assigned to them by astronomers in ancient Greece. The mathematician Ptolemy, who lived in the 2nd century CE, published a catalogue of 48 constellations, which now make up part of the 88. Other cultures, notably the Egyptians and Chinese, studied the skies and had their own constellations, but these are not recognised on the official list.

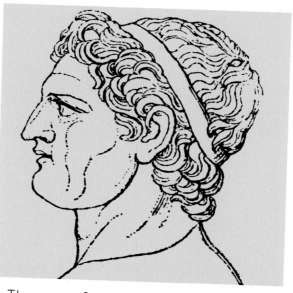

The ancient Greek mathematician Ptolemy

The Plough, highlighted here, is part of Ursa Major.

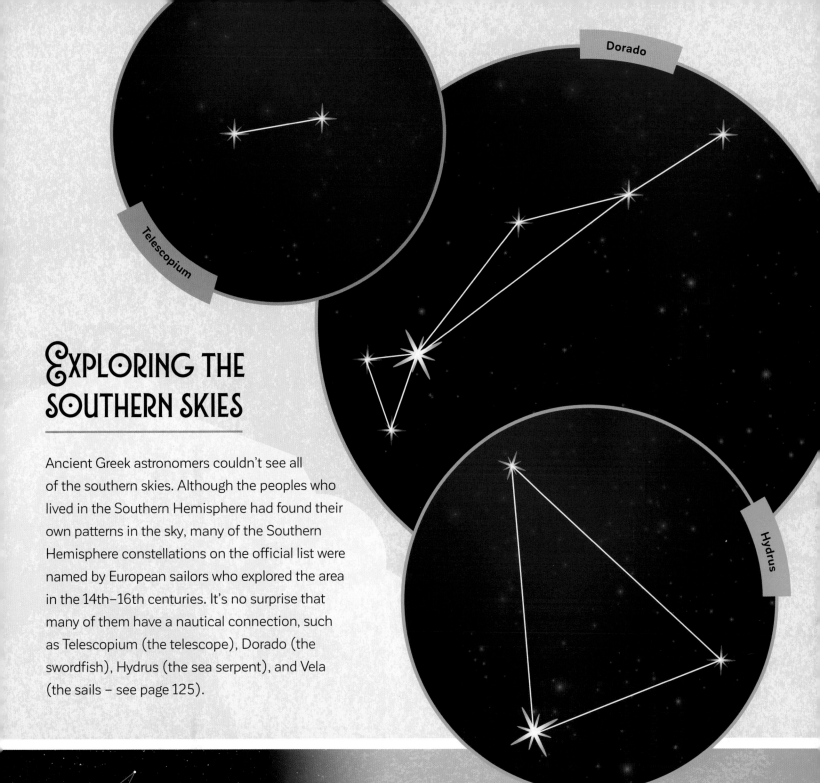

Dorado

Telescopium

Hydrus

Exploring the Southern Skies

Ancient Greek astronomers couldn't see all of the southern skies. Although the peoples who lived in the Southern Hemisphere had found their own patterns in the sky, many of the Southern Hemisphere constellations on the official list were named by European sailors who explored the area in the 14th–16th centuries. It's no surprise that many of them have a nautical connection, such as Telescopium (the telescope), Dorado (the swordfish), Hydrus (the sea serpent), and Vela (the sails – see page 125).

Asterism or Constellation?

It's one of the most recognisable shapes in the sky, but the Plough is not a constellation – at least, not on its own. It's part of a larger grouping of stars known as Ursa Major, or the Great Bear. Ursa Major is one of the 88 official constellations, but the Plough is something called an asterism. An asterism is a pattern of stars that's not on the official list. It can be a small section of a constellation, or it can be a pattern formed by stars from two or more different constellations.

THE ZODIAC

There are constellations in every part of the sky, but the ones along the ecliptic (below) have always been seen as a bit special. This is because the Sun visits each of them on its yearly journey. There are 13 constellations along the ecliptic, and 12 of them form what we know as the zodiac. You can see the relative positions of all the constellations by looking at the star maps on pages 46–47.

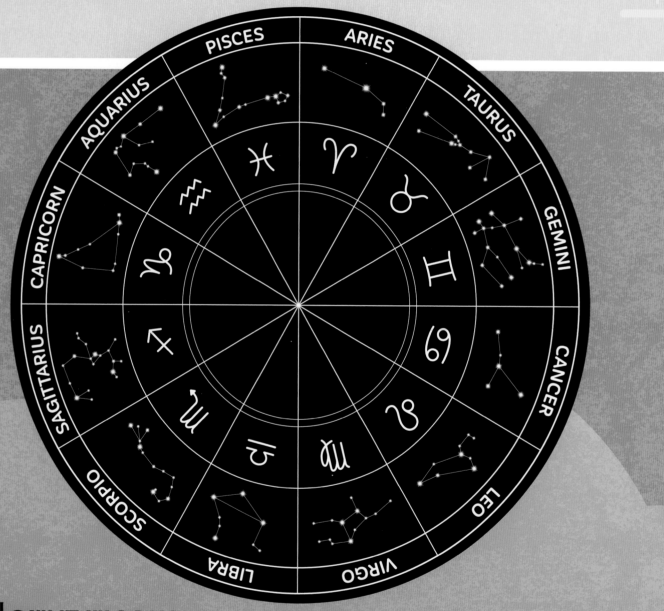

HOW IT WORKS

If stars were visible during the day, at the same time as the Sun, over the course of one year you would see the Sun move through the zodiac constellations, spending about a month in each. Some people believe that the sign the Sun was in when you were born will affect your life. However, the zodiac was set up thousands of years ago, and wobbles in Earth's axis mean that the actual positions of the constellations no longer match up with the traditional dates for each sign.

Aries

Aries is the first of the zodiac constellations, because the Sun appeared there at the spring equinox. To people in the Northern Hemisphere, this day marked the start of the new year, as the Sun awoke from the winter. The constellation represents a ram with a golden fleece from Greek myths. Two of the stars (Hamal and Sheratan) are fairly bright, making it easy to find. With a telescope, you can see that the third-brightest star, Mesarthim, is actually a double star.

FACT FILE

NAME: Aries
REPRESENTS: a ram
VISIBLE: along the ecliptic
BRIGHTEST STAR: Hamal

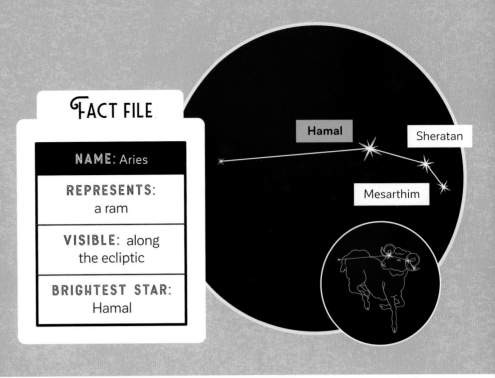

Hamal

Sheratan

Mesarthim

Taurus

The constellation Taurus represents a bull that the Greek god Zeus changed into. The stars form the V-shape of a bull's head, with two long horns. The star Aldebaran is very bright, with a distinct reddish-orange colour. It is a red giant (see page 137) that is nearing the end of its life. The face is made up of stars that are part of a cluster known as the Hyades. The most prominent star cluster in the sky, the Pleiades, or Seven Sisters, is also in Taurus (see pages 130–131).

FACT FILE

NAME: Taurus
REPRESENTS: a bull
VISIBLE: along the ecliptic
BRIGHTEST STAR: Aldebaran

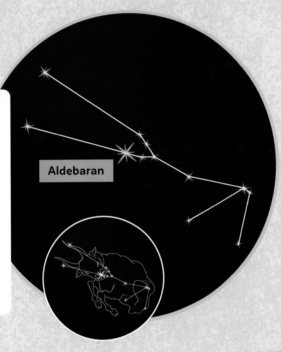

Aldebaran

Gemini

The two brightest stars in this constellation represent the twins Castor and Pollux from Greek mythology. In the stories, Pollux was immortal while Castor was not, and when Castor was killed in battle, Pollux begged to share his immortality with him. So Castor joined his twin brother in the sky! The constellation is made of two roughly parallel lines of stars, each one representing one of the brothers. The stars Castor and Pollux are the heads.

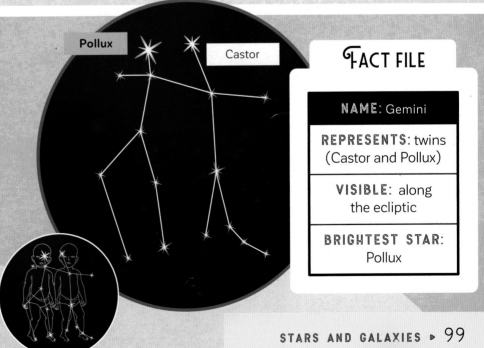

Pollux

Castor

FACT FILE

NAME: Gemini
REPRESENTS: twins (Castor and Pollux)
VISIBLE: along the ecliptic
BRIGHTEST STAR: Pollux

A ZOO IN THE SKY

The word 'zodiac' comes from the Greek *zodiakos kyklos*, meaning 'circle of animals'. (The Greek word *zoion*, meaning 'animal', is where we get the words zoo and zoology from.) The zodiac gets this name because the majority of its constellations, like Cancer and Leo, represent animals. Gemini, Virgo and Aquarius are humans, and Libra is a set of scales.

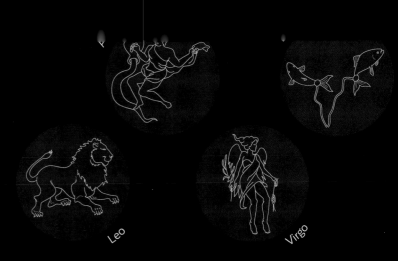

Leo

Virgo

CANCER

Though it can be seen from both hemispheres, depending on the time of year, Cancer is one of the hardest zodiac constellations to spot. It is made up of five main stars, and none of them are particularly bright. According to Greek myth, the goddess Hera sent a crab to the rescue of a monster called the Hydra (see page 122), when the legendary hero Heracles (see page 111) was trying to kill it. The crab didn't succeed, and got squashed when Heracles stepped on it, but Hera rewarded it for its efforts by placing it in the sky. Not a bad result for a failure!

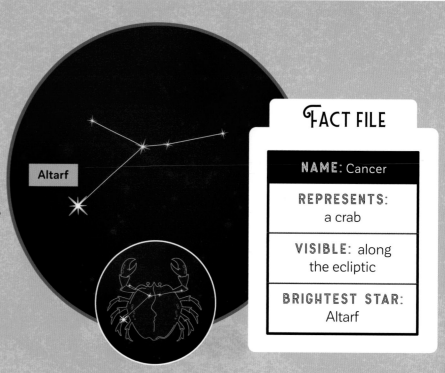

Altarf

FACT FILE

NAME: Cancer
REPRESENTS: a crab
VISIBLE: along the ecliptic
BRIGHTEST STAR: Altarf

LEO

The constellation of Leo also has links to Heracles – it represents the fierce Nemean lion, which the Greek hero killed. Part of Leo looks like a backwards question mark, with the brightest star, Regulus, at the bottom. This shape, often known as 'the sickle', represents the lion's head, with Regulus as its heart. Three other stars make up the rest of the lion's body. This group of stars was seen as a lion by several different ancient cultures. But some saw it as a horse, and others connected the sickle to different stars to make a mountain lion with a curling tail.

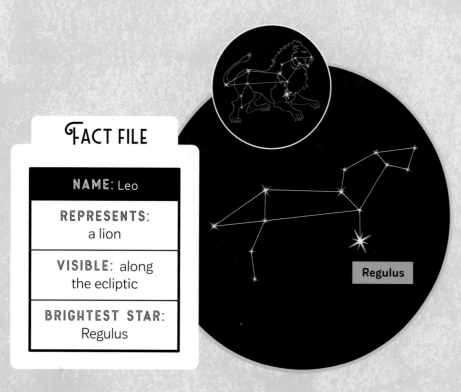

Regulus

FACT FILE

NAME: Leo
REPRESENTS: a lion
VISIBLE: along the ecliptic
BRIGHTEST STAR: Regulus

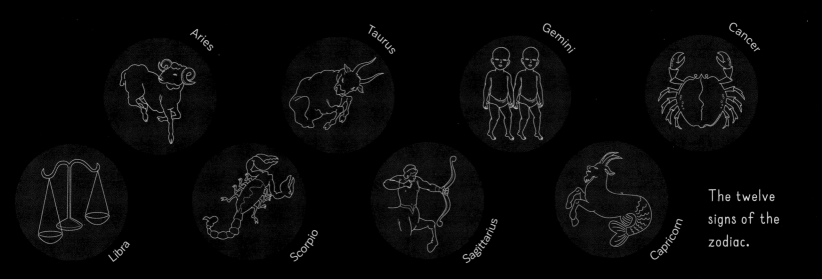

Aries

Taurus

Gemini

Cancer

Libra

Scorpio

Sagittarius

Capricorn

The twelve signs of the zodiac.

Virgo

Virgo is a very large constellation, covering a big area of the sky, but only one of its stars is really bright, so you may struggle to spot the rest of it. This star, called Spica, is actually a double star, or binary star – two close stars that orbit around the same centre of gravity. The bigger of the two produces about 12,000 times more light than our Sun! The second-brightest star, Porrima, is also a binary star, and its two stars are far enough apart that you may be able to see them both with a telescope. The stars in Virgo make up the shape of a young woman, but there are many different stories about who this woman might actually be.

FACT FILE

NAME: Virgo
REPRESENTS: a young woman
VISIBLE: along the ecliptic
BRIGHTEST STAR: Spica

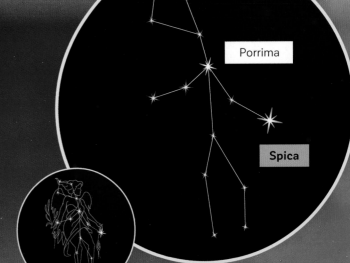

Porrima

Spica

Spica

Spica, the brightest star in Virgo's constellation, is easy to spot in the night sky.

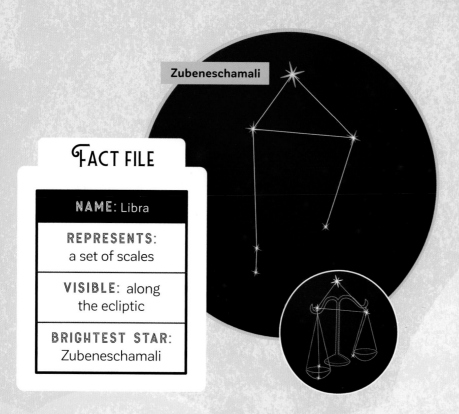

Zubeneschamali

FACT FILE

NAME: Libra
REPRESENTS: a set of scales
VISIBLE: along the ecliptic
BRIGHTEST STAR: Zubeneschamali

LIBRA

Libra is another tricky constellation to spot, as it is fairly small and dim. It is meant to represent a set of scales, but the Arab astronomers who named its stars saw it as the claw of the scorpion in the neighbouring constellation. Their name for the brightest star, Zubeneschamali, literally means 'northern claw'. This star is unusual because it has a slight green tint, though this is hard to see. If you can find Scorpius (see right and page 47), you can use it to find Libra. Libra's three brightest stars form a triangular bucket shape, with the open side pointing to the head of Scorpius.

SAGITTARIUS

Sagittarius represents a fierce centaur (the half-man, half-horse creature from Greek mythology), shooting a bow and arrow. His arrow is pointing at Antares, the heart of the scorpion (see above right). However, many people see some of this constellation's stars as something much less warlike: a teapot! Eight stars make up this asterism. On a dark night, you can see star clouds appearing to emerge from the spout, like steam. If you look past Sagittarius, you are staring into the centre of the Milky Way.

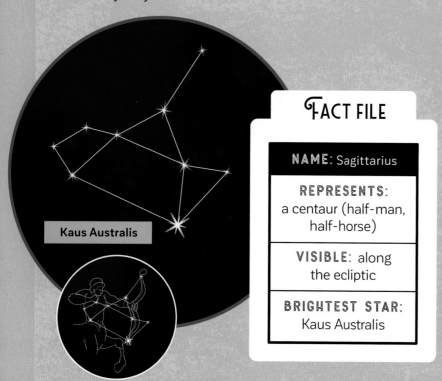

Kaus Australis

FACT FILE

NAME: Sagittarius
REPRESENTS: a centaur (half-man, half-horse)
VISIBLE: along the ecliptic
BRIGHTEST STAR: Kaus Australis

Artist's impression of the supermassive black hole at the heart of the Milky Way

Scorpius

Scorpius is fairly easy to spot – a long, curving string of bright stars that represents a scorpion. In Greek mythology, the scorpion killed the hunter Orion, and the two constellations seem to chase each other across the sky. The bright, reddish star called Antares is the scorpion's heart, while other bright stars form the animal's head. Antares is a type of star known as a red supergiant, and its diameter is about 850 times larger than the Sun's! If it were sitting in the middle of our Solar System, it would engulf the four rocky planets, and almost reach Jupiter.

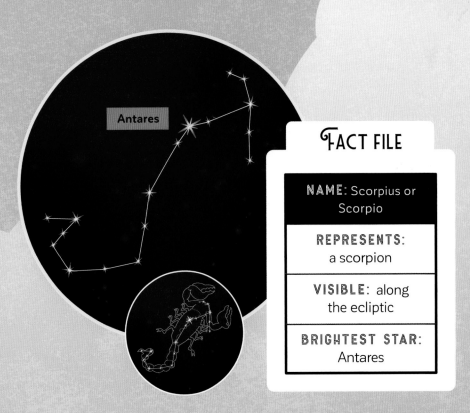

Antares

FACT FILE

NAME: Scorpius or Scorpio	
REPRESENTS: a scorpion	
VISIBLE: along the ecliptic	
BRIGHTEST STAR: Antares	

The Centre of the Galaxy

Many galaxies have a black hole at the centre, and the Milky Way is one such galaxy. A black hole is a relatively small area with enormous mass, which produces gravity so strong that nothing – not even light – can escape. Our galaxy's central black hole lies in the constellation of Sagittarius. The American astronomer Andrea Ghez shared the Nobel Prize in 2020 for proving the existence of the black hole at the centre of the Milky Way. Although we can't see it, it produces radio waves, and astronomers know this radio source as Sagittarius A* (often known as Sag A Star).

CAPRICORNUS

The Babylonians in ancient Mesopotamia thought that this grouping of stars looked like a cross between a goat and a fish. They associated this creature with their water god, Ea. The Greeks told stories of the god Pan, who changed himself into a goat-fish as he jumped into the River Nile in an attempt to escape the giant Typhon. Looking today, you'll see that this faint constellation is shaped a bit like an upside-down version of the badges worn in *Star Trek*! It has no particularly bright stars, but you may be able to pick out the three stars at the points of the triangle.

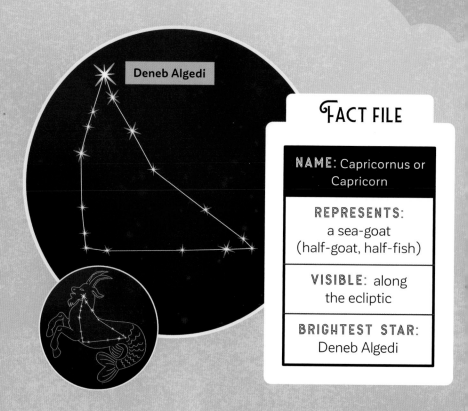

Deneb Algedi

FACT FILE

NAME: Capricornus or Capricorn
REPRESENTS: a sea-goat (half-goat, half-fish)
VISIBLE: along the ecliptic
BRIGHTEST STAR: Deneb Algedi

PISCES

Like Capricorn and Aquarius, Pisces is faint and hard to see, especially in cities, where electric lights will drown out even its brightest stars. Although the Babylonians saw it as a swallow, it is often depicted as a pair of fish, tied together with a rope. A Greek myth tells the story of the goddess Aphrodite and her son, Eros. They were being chased by Typhon, and they ended up on a river bank. They tied themselves together with a rope before turning themselves into fish, then jumped in. The rope kept them from becoming separated as they were swept away.

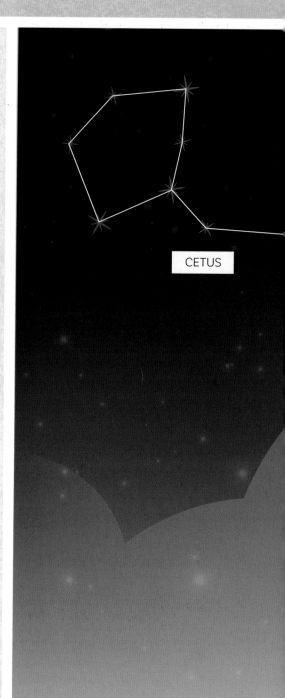

CETUS

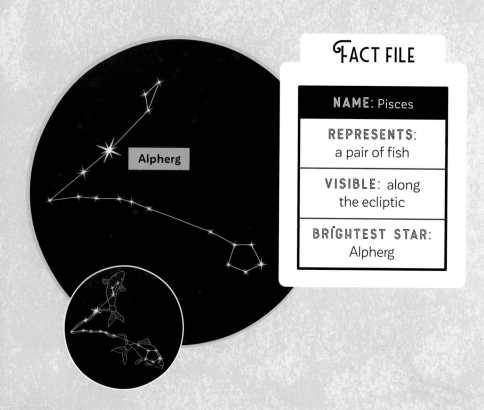

Alpherg

FACT FILE

NAME: Pisces
REPRESENTS: a pair of fish
VISIBLE: along the ecliptic
BRIGHTEST STAR: Alpherg

Aquarius

This constellation covers a fairly large area of the sky, but its stars are relatively faint, making it harder to spot. Aquarius is meant to look like a human figure carrying a jug of water, and the four stars that form the jug make a diamond shape that you can look for. To the Chinese, the stars that form the stream of water flowing out of this jar represent the army of Yu-Lin – foot soldiers from the northern parts of the empire. Astronomers have found several stars here with planets orbiting them. They have also discovered a helix-shaped nebula (see pages 142–143).

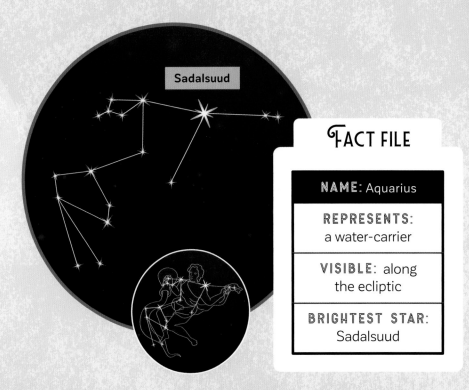

Sadalsuud

FACT FILE

NAME: Aquarius
REPRESENTS: a water-carrier
VISIBLE: along the ecliptic
BRIGHTEST STAR: Sadalsuud

DELPHINUS

PISCIS AUSTRINUS

The Sea of the Heavens

Capricorn, Aquarius and Pisces are all in the same area of the sky – a region often known as 'the Sea'. It is home to several constellations with a watery theme, including Cetus (the whale), Delphinus (the dolphin), and Piscis Austrinus (the southern fish). These constellations were all known to astronomers in the ancient Middle East. They may have become associated with water because the Sun passed through them at the same time of year that marked the rainy season.

Other Interpretations

The ancient Egyptians used the zodiac, but they replaced the mythical figures we know with their own gods and goddesses. So Aries (the ram) became the god Amun (who was often portrayed with a ram's head), and Taurus (the bull) was replaced with the bull-god, Apis. The Hindu zodiac is also very similar, though it is measured slightly differently. The symbols have different names but familiar meanings, such as twins, lion and crab. The main difference is Capricorn, which is known as Makara and is represented by a sea monster that looks like a crocodile.

To the ancient Egyptians, Aries the ram was the god Amun, represented by these giant statues built around 380 BCE.

The Chinese Zodiac

In the Chinese zodiac, each year (rather than each month) is represented by an animal, such as an ox, tiger, rabbit or monkey (see left). This system is not based on the movement of constellations –instead, it is linked to the movement of Jupiter. The planet Jupiter takes just under 12 years to complete one orbit of the Sun, and during that time it moves through the Chinese zodiac at a rate of about one sign per year.

OPHIUCHUS

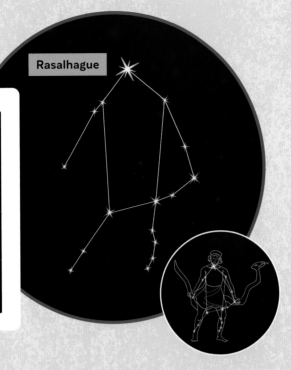

FACT FILE

NAME: Ophiuchus	
REPRESENTS: a man holding a snake	
VISIBLE: along the ecliptic	
BRIGHTEST STAR: Rasalhague	

Rasalhague

There is a 13th constellation along the ecliptic. Ophiuchus is between Scorpius and Sagittarius. It's not considered to be a sign of the zodiac, but it's still an interesting constellation! Some say it represents the Greek god Apollo; others say it's the legendary healer Asclepius. To Islamic astronomers, it was Al-Hawwa, the snake-charmer (their name for its brightest star, Rasalhague, means 'head of the serpent-charmer'). Ophiuchus was the site of a supernova in 1604, which was visible to the naked eye.

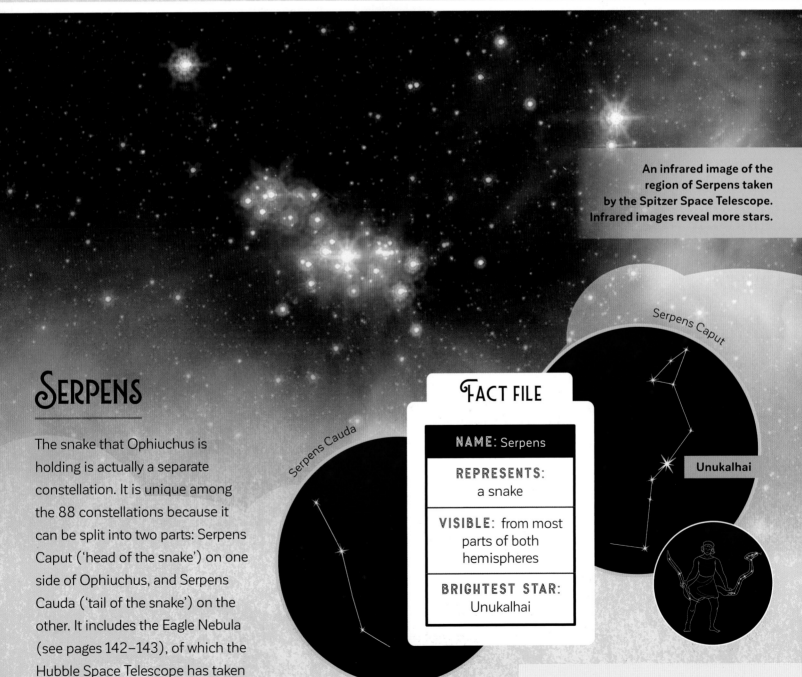

An infrared image of the region of Serpens taken by the Spitzer Space Telescope. Infrared images reveal more stars.

SERPENS

The snake that Ophiuchus is holding is actually a separate constellation. It is unique among the 88 constellations because it can be split into two parts: Serpens Caput ('head of the snake') on one side of Ophiuchus, and Serpens Cauda ('tail of the snake') on the other. It includes the Eagle Nebula (see pages 142–143), of which the Hubble Space Telescope has taken stunning images.

Serpens Caput

Serpens Cauda

Unukalhai

FACT FILE

NAME: Serpens	
REPRESENTS: a snake	
VISIBLE: from most parts of both hemispheres	
BRIGHTEST STAR: Unukalhai	

OTHER CONSTELLATIONS

The constellations of the zodiac make up a relatively narrow belt around the celestial sphere. There are a host of other constellations above and below it. Those nearest the poles are only ever visible from their own hemisphere. But most are visible from both, though usually at different times of year. The closer you are to the Equator, the bigger the range of constellations that you'll be able to see.

Ursa Major

The Plough (see page 97) is part of a larger constellation called Ursa Major, or the 'Great Bear'. In Greek mythology, the constellation represents Callisto, who was turned into a bear after having a son with the god Zeus. The Plough's seven bright stars are the bear's tail and rear, while the stars in its head and legs are much fainter. The middle star of the handle is actually two stars very close together – Mizar and Alcor. If you have sharp eyes you might be able to see them both, and this was used as a vision test in ancient times. A distant galaxy called the Cigar Galaxy is located in Ursa Major (see page 153).

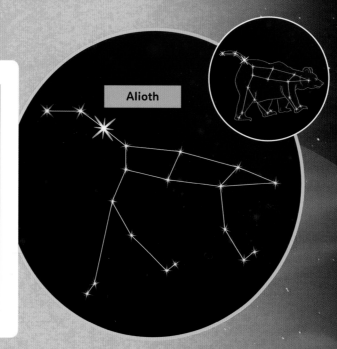

Alioth

Plough

FACT FILE

NAME: Ursa Major

REPRESENTS:
a bear

VISIBLE: from the Northern Hemisphere and northerly parts of the Southern Hemisphere

BRIGHTEST STAR:
Alioth

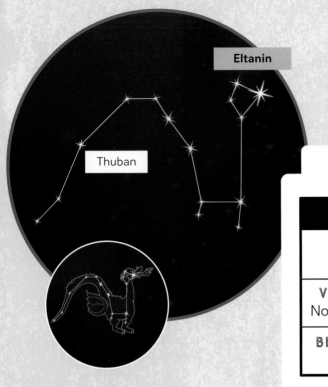

DRACO

Thanks to its position near the North Pole, Draco is visible from the Northern Hemisphere all year round, though it can only be seen from the very northernmost parts of the Southern Hemisphere. In fact, about 6,000 years ago, its star Thuban was used as the pole star. Back then, it was closer to Earth's North Pole than Polaris was. The constellation represents a legendary Greek dragon called Ladon, who guarded an orchard full of magical golden apples. This patch of sky is home to the Cat's Eye Nebula (see pages 142–143), one of the first nebulas of its type to be discovered.

FACT FILE

NAME: Draco

REPRESENTS: a dragon

VISIBLE: from the Northern Hemisphere

BRIGHTEST STAR: Eltanin

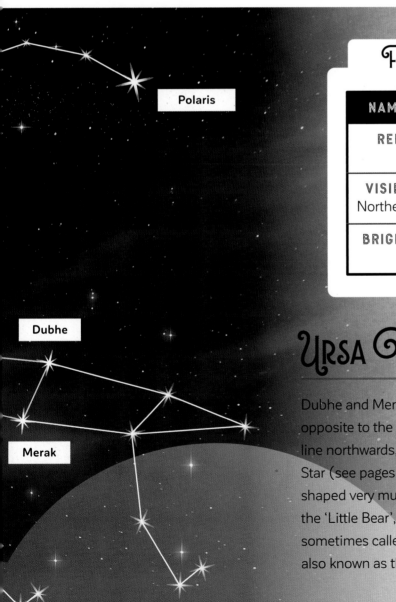

FACT FILE

NAME: Ursa Minor

REPRESENTS: a bear

VISIBLE: from the Northern Hemisphere

BRIGHTEST STAR: Polaris

URSA MINOR

Dubhe and Merak are the two stars that make up the side of the Plough opposite to the handle. If you imagine a line connecting them, then follow that line northwards, you'll reach a bright star called Polaris, also known as the Pole Star (see pages 34–35). Polaris is the tip of the tail of a smaller constellation shaped very much like the Plough, but upside down. This is Ursa Minor, or the 'Little Bear', said to represent Arcas, the son of Callisto and Zeus. It is sometimes called the 'Little Dipper' because of its similarity to the Plough, also known as the 'Big Dipper'.

BOÖTES

This constellation gets its name from a Greek word meaning 'ox-driver' or 'ploughman'. In some legends, Boötes is the name of the man who invented the plough, and he was turned into a constellation as a reward. Its position in the sky means that the ploughman can push along the plough that makes up part of Ursa Major. Its bright stars, arranged in a pattern that looks like a kite, make it fairly easy to spot. Arcturus, at the point of its narrow end, is one of the brightest stars in the night sky. It is a giant star with an orange colour that is fairly obvious to the naked eye.

FACT FILE

NAME: Boötes

REPRESENTS: a farmer

VISIBLE: from the Northern Hemisphere and part of the Southern Hemisphere

BRIGHTEST STAR: Arcturus

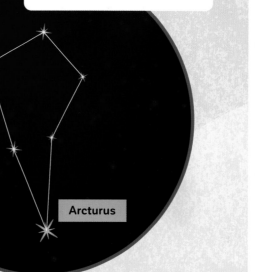

Arcturus

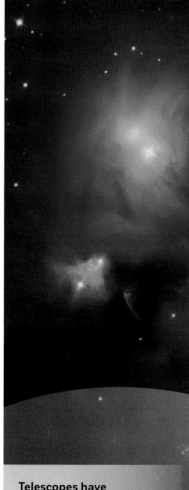

Telescopes have identified a star-forming region known as a molecular cloud within Corona Australis.

CORONA BOREALIS

With its distinctive 'U' shape, this constellation is often said to represent a crown. According to Greek mythology, the god Dionysos gave this crown to the mortal princess Ariadne when he married her. One version of the story says that he threw the crown into the sky to prove he was a god! To the Welsh, this constellation is a castle rather than a crown – the home of the mythical Lady Arianrhod. To some Native American peoples, the seven stars represent a semi-circle of tents.

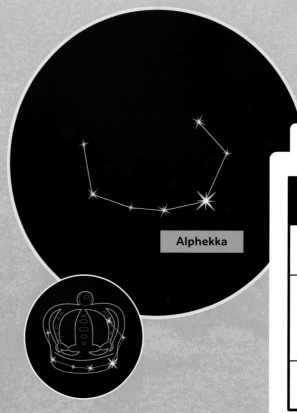

Alphekka

FACT FILE

NAME: Corona Borealis

REPRESENTS: a crown

VISIBLE: from the Northern Hemisphere and part of the Southern Hemisphere

BRIGHTEST STAR: Alphekka

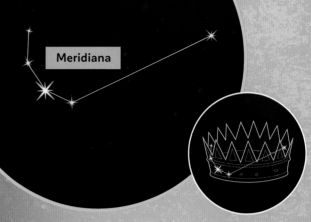

FACT FILE

NAME:	Corona Australis
REPRESENTS:	a crown
VISIBLE:	from the Southern Hemisphere and part of the Northern Hemisphere
BRIGHTEST STAR:	Meridiana

CORONA AUSTRALIS

Corona Borealis has a two-part name to set it apart from another 'U'-shaped constellation named after a crown: Corona Australis. This 'southern crown' is visible from all of the Southern Hemisphere and parts of the Northern Hemisphere. To the Chinese, its curve represented a turtle's shell. To some of Australia's aboriginal peoples, it's a boomerang. Other cultures have seen it as an ostrich nest or as people sitting around a fire.

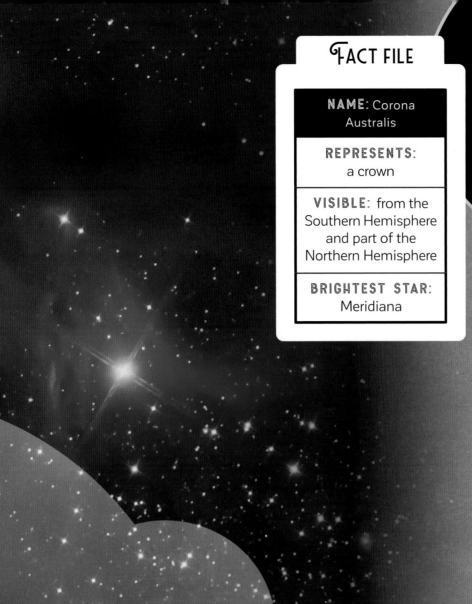

FACT FILE

NAME:	Hercules
REPRESENTS:	the legendary hero Heracles
VISIBLE:	from the Northern Hemisphere (April–November) and the Southern Hemisphere (June–September)
BRIGHTEST STAR:	Kornephoros

HERCULES

The constellation of Hercules, found next to Corona Borealis, is big but not very bright. Its central feature is an asterism called the Keystone, made of four stars arranged in a roughly square shape. (If you want to be picky, it's actually a trapezium!) This is the torso of the Greek hero Heracles, who was called Hercules by the Romans. He was famous for his strength and bravery. The stars coming out from the Keystone form his arms and legs. In the legends, Heracles killed the dragon Ladon, and his constellation looks as though it is stepping on the head of Draco (see pages 46, 108–109). It's home to a stunning globular star cluster (see pages 132–133).

LYRA

Lyra is a small constellation, but it includes the brilliant blue star Vega, which produces over 50 times more light than the Sun! Even from its position 26 light years away, it is still one of the brightest stars in the sky. It is the cornerstone of this small constellation that represents a stringed instrument called a lyre, which the Greek god Apollo gave to his son, Orpheus. Lyra's six main stars form a rough diamond (or parallelogram) shape, with the last two stars forming the prongs at the top. The constellation includes a ring-shaped nebula (see pages 140–141).

(see pages 140–141)

FACT FILE

NAME: Lyra

REPRESENTS: a lyre

VISIBLE: from the Northern Hemisphere and part of the Southern Hemisphere

BRIGHTEST STAR: Vega

FACT FILE

NAME: Aquila

REPRESENTS: an eagle

VISIBLE: from the Northern Hemisphere and most of the Southern Hemisphere, season dependent

BRIGHTEST STAR: Altair

Vega

The three bright stars of the Summer Triangle stand out against the Milky Way.

DENEB

CYGNUS

A swan with wings outstretched, soaring through the sky, is a truly majestic sight. And the constellation of Cygnus is meant to show exactly that! The five brightest stars form a clear T-shaped asterism often known as the Northern Cross. Fainter stars continue off from the crosspiece, forming the swan's wings. The bright supergiant star Deneb forms the tail – not surprising, given that Deneb is the Arabic word for 'tail'! To the Dakota people of North America, this cross shape is a salamander, and in Mongolia it's a bow and arrow.

FACT FILE

NAME: Cygnus

REPRESENTS: a swan

VISIBLE: from the Northern Hemisphere and most of the Southern Hemisphere, season dependent

BRIGHTEST STAR: Deneb

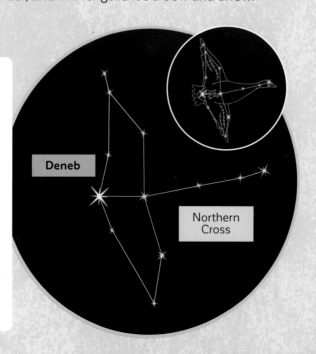

Deneb

Northern Cross

Aquila

Cygnus is not the only starry bird flying across the night sky – the neighbouring constellation Aquila represents an eagle in flight. If you can find Cygnus, look for Aquila 'flying' parallel to it, towards Scorpius. Its brightest star, Altair, spins so fast that it has a slightly flattened shape, rather than being completely spherical. In the Chinese love story of Niulang and Zhinu (see pages 88–89), Altair represents the cowherd Niulang, and Vega, in Lyra, is his wife, Zhinu. They are separated by the 'river' of the Milky Way.

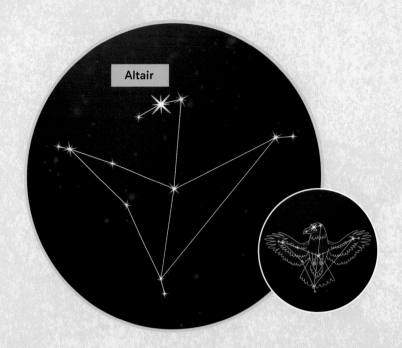

Altair

VEGA

The Summer Triangle

The brightest stars in each of these three constellations – Vega, Deneb and Altair – make a roughly triangular shape in the sky. This asterism is known as the Summer Triangle. (It's more of an isosceles triangle than an equilateral triangle, with Deneb and Vega a bit closer to each other than they are to Altair.) It can be seen for most of the year from the Northern Hemisphere, but in summer it's directly overhead. This is winter in the Southern Hemisphere, and stargazers there can see the triangle low above the northern horizon. Locating the triangle makes it easier to locate the constellations.

ALTAIR

PEGASUS

Not to be outdone by the swan and the eagle found in the stars, the constellation of Pegasus represents a winged horse. When looking for it, stargazers often start with the asterism known as the Great Square of Pegasus – made up of four bright stars that form a rough square shape. The brightest of them, Alpheratz, is officially part of the neighbouring constellation of Andromeda. The star diagonally across from it is Markab. It represents the saddle, and a string of stars extend from it to form the horse's neck.

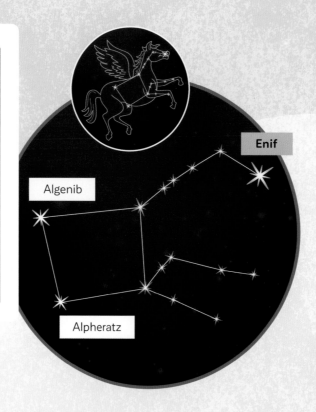

Enif

Algenib

Alpheratz

ANDROMEDA

In Greek mythology, Andromeda was the princess who was chained to a rock as an offering to a sea monster (see pages 12–13). In the constellation that bears her name, the stars show her in that position, standing with her arms outstretched, though in the sky she appears upside down. The bright star Alpheratz, which is one corner of the Great Square of Pegasus, forms her head. Try to spot the faint smudge of the Andromeda Galaxy (see pages 148–149), near one of the young woman's knees. It is the farthest object that you can see with the naked eye.

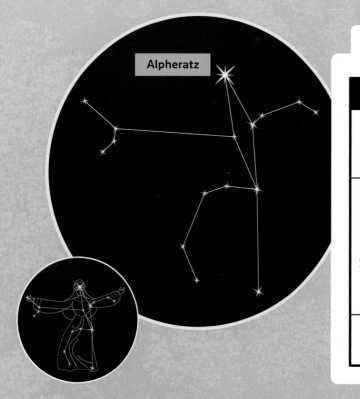

Alpheratz

Perseus contains Algol, which is a double star.

PERSEUS

The bright stars in the constellation of Perseus make it fairly easy to spot, with the star Mirfak at the heart of this constellation. Perseus was one of the greatest heroes in Greek mythology. Other cultures see different arrangements of stars. The Tukano people of the Amazon rainforest see a jaguar or puma, while the Sami people of northern Scandinavia see an elk. From mid-July to mid-August the Perseid meteor shower is visible, when Earth passes through a trail of debris left by comet Swift-Tuttle. The meteors streaking across the sky appear to radiate out from this area of the sky. Perseus is also the site of a double star cluster (see pages 132–133).

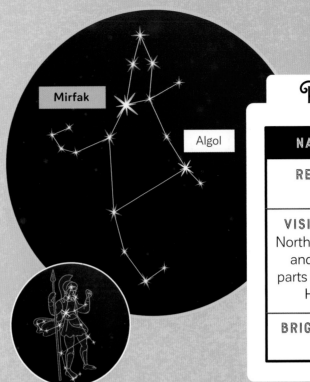

Mirfak

Algol

DOUBLE STARS

The second-brightest star in Perseus is called Algol, which means 'demon star' in Arabic – this is where our word 'ghoul' comes from! Ancient stargazers thought the star was cursed because its brightness changes from day to day. To the Greeks, it was the head of the monster Medusa, who could turn people to stone by looking at them. Astronomers now know that Algol contains two stars revolving around each other, known as an eclipsing binary. One star is fainter than the other, and as it passes in front, it blocks some of the brighter star's light. With Algol, this happens every three days.

ORION

Orion is one of the most famous and easily recognisable constellations in the night sky. Its bright stars make a clear shape that many people see as a human figure. There are two stars representing the shoulders and two more at the knees, with an angled belt of three closely placed stars cinching in the waist. Orion was known to the ancient Greeks as a mighty hunter, who was finally killed by a scorpion (see pages 102–103). Fainter stars form his arms and weapons, including a sword hanging from his belt. The constellation also includes the beautiful Orion Nebula (see pages 140–141).

FACT FILE

NAME: Orion
REPRESENTS: a hunter
VISIBLE: from the Northern Hemisphere and most of the Southern Hemisphere, season dependent
BRIGHTEST STAR: Rigel

Betelgeuse

Rigel

The famous constellation Orion is captured here behind clouds.

Orion's Belt

Orion Nebula

TWO GIANTS

Orion includes two enormous stars: Betelgeuse (which is the shoulder on the left, as you look at it) and Rigel (the knee on the right). If you look closely, you'll see that they have different colours. Betelgeuse is reddish-orange, while Rigel is blue. Both are much bigger than our Sun. Rigel is super-hot, burning through its fuel at a tremendous rate. Betelgeuse is nearing the end of its life and has swelled up to an enormous size. In late 2019 it got noticeably dimmer, and some astronomers thought it might be about to explode. But after a few months it became brighter again. They now think that it 'burped' out a cloud of dust that blocked its light and made it appear dimmer.

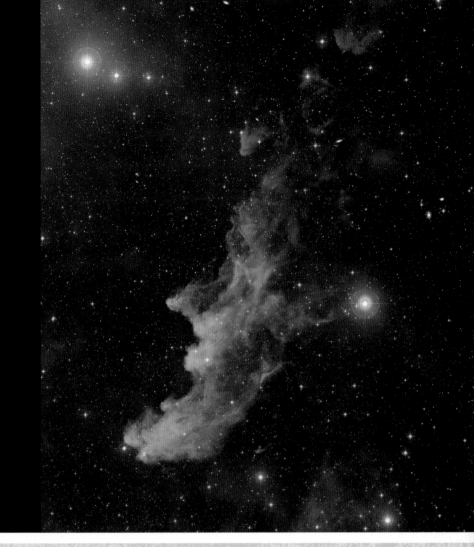

Betelgeuse (top) and Rigel lie either side of the Witch Head Nebula.

OTHER CULTURES

Not everyone looks at Orion's stars and sees a human figure. To the Yokut people of California, the three stars of the belt were the footprints of the god of the flea people, who scared them away when he appeared in the sky. That's why fleas don't bite in winter, when Orion is visible. Korean legend tells of three triplet brothers (the stars of the belt) who guard against evil dragons. In Puerto Rico, the belt stars are known as the Three Wise Men. In Hawaii, the shoulders, knees and belt represent the string game cat's cradle.

POINTING THE WAY

Orion is useful as a pathfinder, pointing the way to other constellations. If you imagine a line connecting the belt stars, from top right to bottom left, and continue following it down, you'll reach the bright star Sirius in the constellation Canis Major (see pages 118–119). Follow that same line in the other direction, and you come close to Aldebaran in Taurus (see pages 98–99). If you imagine a line from Rigel up through Betelgeuse and keep going, you'll reach Alhena, the star at the bottom of Gemini (see pages 98–99). In the Southern Hemisphere, you'll have to reverse these instructions as Orion appears upside down.

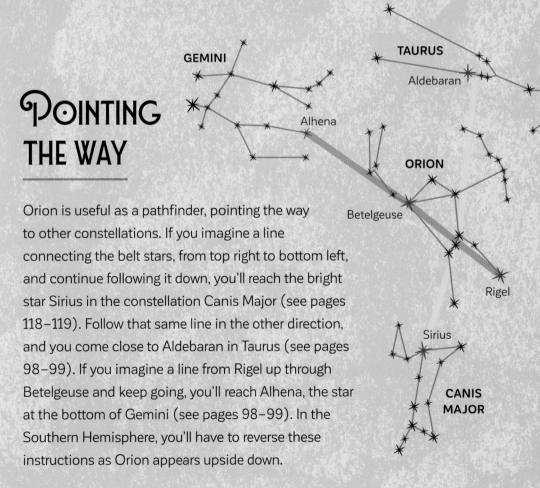

CANIS MAJOR

According to the legends, Orion was accompanied by two hunting dogs when he was alive. In the sky, his constellation is also followed by two loyal dogs. The larger of them is called Canis Major, which just means 'big dog' in Latin. Its brightest star, Sirius, is actually the brightest star in the night sky! It is bigger than the Sun, and only 8.6 light years away. Sirius is part of constellations in many cultures. The Boorong people of Australia use five of the stars in Canis Major to form a rough 'W' shape that represents a wedge-tailed eagle in flight.

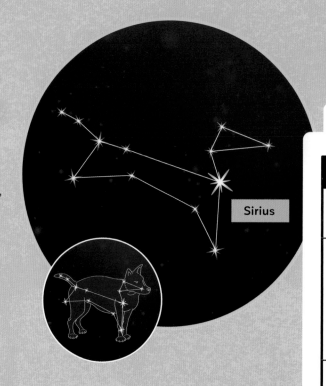

Sirius

WIZARDS IN THE SKY

Many characters in the Harry Potter books are named after stars. Sirius Black is named after the star Sirius, also known as the 'Dog Star' because it is in Canis Major. The character in the book has the ability to shape-shift into a dog, which is appropriate! His cousin, the villain Bellatrix Lestrange, is named after one of the stars in Orion, and the name means 'female warrior'. He has another cousin called Andromeda, and a brother called Regulus.

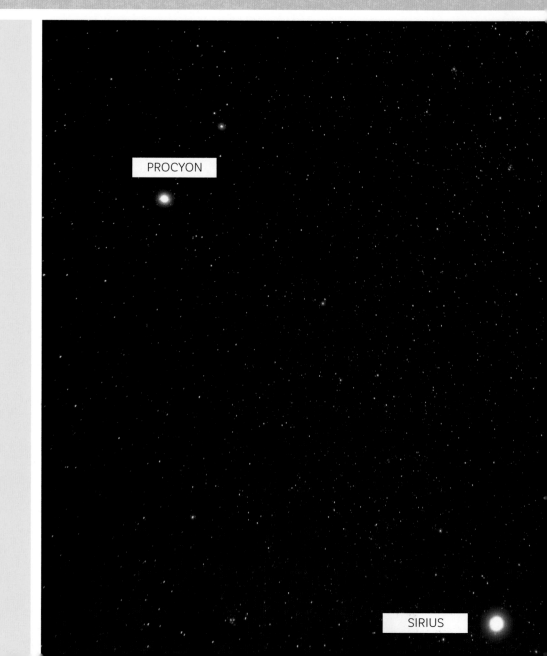

PROCYON

SIRIUS

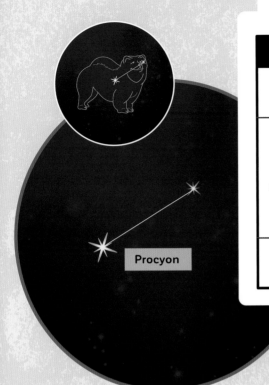

NAME: Canis Minor

REPRESENTS:
a smaller dog

VISIBLE: from all of the Southern Hemisphere and most of the Northern Hemisphere, season dependent

BRIGHTEST STAR:
Procyon

Procyon

CANIS MINOR

The second of Orion's hunting dogs is much smaller – in fact, the shape is represented by just two stars! Another story says that this little dog sits under the table of Castor and Pollux (the Gemini twins – see page 99), waiting for scraps. The ancient Egyptians saw this constellation as the god Anubis, who had the head of a jackal. The bright star Procyon has a name meaning 'before the dog', probably because each night it leads Sirius through the sky. The second star, called Gomeisa, is also fairly bright.

BETELGEUSE

THE WINTER TRIANGLE

Just like Vega, Deneb and Aquila form a Summer Triangle (see pages 112–113), there is also a Winter Triangle (left). It's made up of Sirius, Procyon and Betelgeuse (see pages 116–117). In the Northern Hemisphere, this triangle is visible high in the sky during the winter months. This is summer in the Southern Hemisphere, and stargazers there can see it upside down and lower in the sky. It is a handy way to find constellations.

CASSIOPEIA

Cassiopeia was a queen in Greek mythology and the mother of Andromeda (see pages 114–115). The five main stars in her constellation form a 'W' shape that looks a bit like a crown, but it is actually meant to show her sitting on her throne. You can find it by starting with the Plough in Ursa Major. Follow the line up to Polaris (see pages 108–109) and keep going until you reach Cassiopeia. As the stars rotate around Polaris through the course of the night, Cassiopeia and Ursa Major will remain on opposite sides of the sky.

FACT FILE

NAME: Cassiopeia
REPRESENTS: a woman sitting on a throne
VISIBLE: from all of the Southern Hemisphere and most of the Northern Hemisphere, season dependent
BRIGHTEST STAR: Schedar

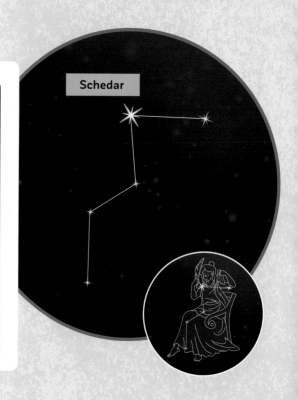

Schedar

FACT FILE

NAME: Cepheus
REPRESENTS: a standing man
VISIBLE: from all of the Southern Hemisphere and most of the Northern Hemisphere, season dependent
BRIGHTEST STAR: Alderamin

The Cepheus constellation in the night sky

DELTA CEPHEI

ALDERAMIN

MU CEPHEI

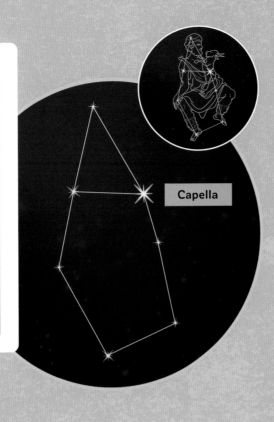

Capella

AURIGA

The main stars that make up Auriga form a rough hexagon. The constellation is meant to represent a charioteer, though he has no horse. In many depictions he is holding the reins with his right hand and baby goats with his left. The brightest star, Capella, is actually a pair of yellow stars similar to our Sun (but about two and a half times as big), accompanied by a pair of smaller, dimmer stars. Capella's name means 'little goat'. The ancient Babylonians saw it as part of a constellation that represented a shepherd's crook, while Islamic astronomers saw Auriga as a herd of goats.

CEPHEUS

In Greek mythology, Cepheus was the king of Ethiopia, and Cassiopeia's husband. His constellation is shaped like a box with a triangle on top. Its brightest star, Alderamin, is at the bottom right corner of the box. Just to the left and a bit below Alderamin is the star Mu Cephei, which has a very distinct reddish tint. But the most interesting star in Cepheus is actually Delta Cephei. It was the first of a class of stars called Cepheid variables to be discovered, back in 1784.

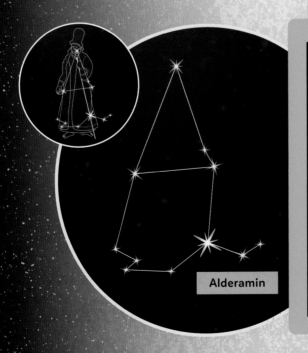

Alderamin

HENRIETTA SWAN LEAVITT

Henrietta Swan Leavitt was a 'human computer' at the Harvard Observatory (see page 93). She studied Cepheid variable stars, which brighten and dim on a regular cycle, and found that the length of a star's cycle is related to how bright the star is. By comparing that measurement with how bright a star appears from Earth, astronomers could work out how far away it is. This allowed Edwin Hubble to prove that the Andromeda Galaxy was outside the Milky Way (see pages 22–23).

BORN: 1868, Massachusetts, United States	DIED: 1921, Massachusetts, United States

JOHANN BAYER

Hydrus and Tucana appear in a star atlas called *Uranometria* (below), first published in 1603 by German astronomer Johann Bayer. The book included more stars than previous atlases did, including Petrus Plancius' new constellations as seen from the Southern Hemisphere (see below right). Bayer is remembered today for inventing the system of naming stars with a Greek letter and their constellation, in order of their brightness.

BORN:	DIED:
1572, Rain, Germany	1625, Augsburg, Germany

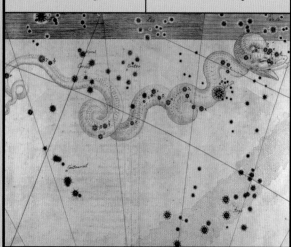

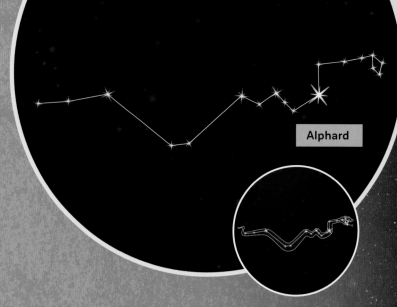

Alphard

HYDRA

In terms of the amount of sky it covers, Hydra is the biggest of the 88 constellations. It stretches over 100 degrees – that's more than half the sky! Hydra runs all the way from Libra (see page 102) in the south to Cancer (see page 100) in the north. It represents a many-headed monster from Greek mythology. Every time Heracles cut off one of its heads, another would grow back. The constellation only has one head – a small ring of five not-very-bright stars. The brightest star, Alphard, is known as the 'heart' of the serpent.

FACT FILE

NAME: Hydrus	
REPRESENTS: a sea snake	
VISIBLE: from all of the Southern Hemisphere and the most southerly parts of the Northern Hemisphere	
BRIGHTEST STAR: Beta Hydri	

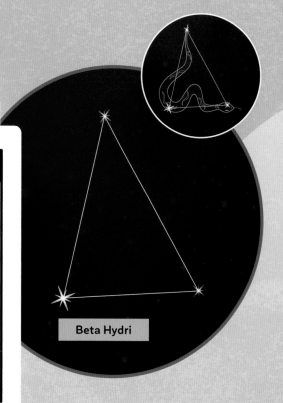

Beta Hydri

HYDRUS

Thanks to their similar names, it would be easy to confuse the constellations Hydra and Hydrus, but they are nothing alike. Hydrus is much smaller, and it is really only visible from the Southern Hemisphere. It circles the South Pole in the same way that Ursa Minor circles the North Pole (see pages 108–109). Astronomers have found four stars in Hydrus that have exoplanets circling them, including one that might have up to nine planets in orbit around it.

The constellation of Hydra stretches right across the night sky like a giant sea serpent.

TUCANA

Tucana, or 'the Toucan', is another southern
constellation, though it is visible a bit further
north of the Equator than Hydrus is. It is one
of 12 southern constellations created by the
Dutch astronomer Petrus Plancius in the late
1500s. He based them on the observations of
Dutch sailors and explorers. Plancius named
many of the new constellations after animals,
and Tucana is grouped together with Grus (the
crane), Pavo (the peacock) and Phoenix as the
'southern birds'. None of Tucana's stars are
particularly bright, but it is the location of the
Small Magellanic Cloud (see pages 150–151).

FACT FILE

NAME: Tucana

REPRESENTS:
a toucan

VISIBLE: from all of
the Southern
Hemisphere and the
southern parts of the
Northern Hemisphere

BRIGHTEST STAR:
Alpha Tucanae

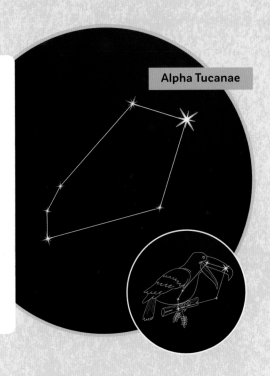
Alpha Tucanae

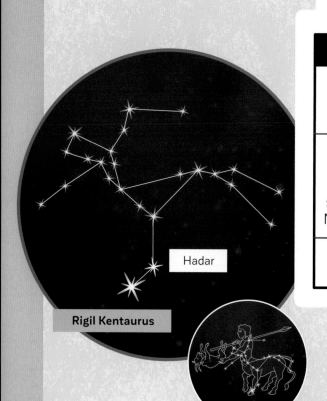

Rigil Kentaurus

Hadar

CENTAURUS

This large constellation is a familiar sight in the Southern Hemisphere. Back in the time of the Babylonians, it was visible further north than it is today. They saw it as a four-legged bison with a human head and torso. The Greeks saw it as a half-man, half-horse creature called a centaur. Its brightest star, Rigil Kentaurus, is also known as Alpha Centauri. For many years, astronomers believed this was the closest star to our Sun, at 4.37 light years away. They later discovered that it was a double star. In 1915, Scottish astronomer Robert Innes discovered a very faint third star in the system. This third star is the closest, so it is called Proxima Centauri (meaning 'nearest star of Centaurus'). The constellation of Centaurus also includes an enormous star cluster called Omega Centauri (see pages 134–135).

CRUX

Also known as the Southern Cross, Crux is the smallest of the 88 constellations and is surrounded on three sides by the much larger Centaurus. In fact, until 1679 it was considered to be part of Centaurus. Although it's small, its four main stars are bright and form a clear cross-shaped pattern, making it easy to spot. Just look for the very bright stars Rigil Kentaurus and Hadar (also known as Alpha and Beta Centauri), which are in the legs of Centaurus. Follow them to the right and you'll reach Crux. This constellation appears on the flags of Australia, New Zealand, Brazil, Samoa and Papua New Guinea. It includes the gorgeous Jewel Box Cluster (see pages 134–135), which you can spot with a telescope.

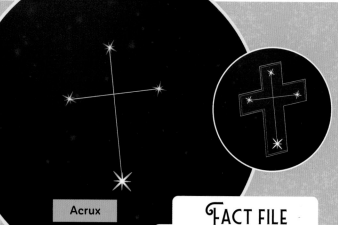

Acrux

The three constellations that were known as Argo Navis

CARINA

Carina represents the keel of a ship called the *Argo*, which carried the legendary Greek hero Jason and his crew on their quest to find the magical Golden Fleece. It contains a stunning star cluster (see pages 134–135) as well as a nebula (see pages 144–145). It also contains Canopus, the second-brightest star in the night sky, after Sirius. Canopus takes its name from a famous navigator in Greek mythology, but the Chinese called it the Old Man of the South Pole – a symbol of happiness and long life. Its location and brightness make it useful for navigating in space, and several spacecraft have been built with special tools for tracking it.

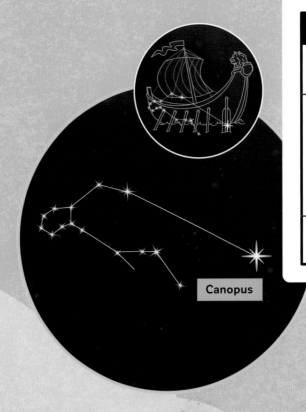

Canopus

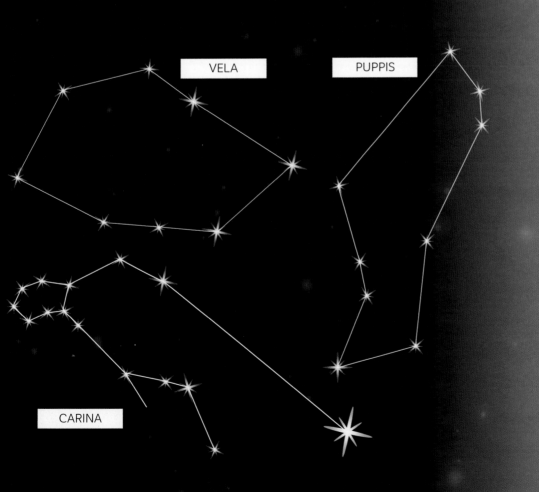

VELA

PUPPIS

CARINA

GOING, GOING, GONE

In his book, the *Almagest*, the ancient Greek astronomer Ptolemy (see pages 96–97) included a constellation that he called Argo Navis ('the ship *Argo*'). But in 1763, the French astronomer Nicolas Louis de Lacaille chopped up this large constellation into three separate ones: Puppis (the poop deck), Vela (the sails) and Carina (the keel). To add insult to injury, thanks to a long-term wobble in Earth's axis, Carina can no longer be seen from Ptolemy's hometown of Alexandria, Egypt. Poor Ptolemy!

CETUS

Cetus has a name meaning 'whale', and it represents the sea monster that Perseus killed in order to save Andromeda (see pages 12–13). You can find it by looking for its brightest star, Deneb Kaitos (meaning 'the tail of the whale'). First find the Great Square of Pegasus (see pages 114–115) and imagine a line leading from Alpheratz through Algenib. Keep going and you'll reach Deneb Kaitos.

Mira

Deneb Kaitos

This barred spiral galaxy lies in the constellation of Cetus.

THE FAINT STAR

The most famous star in Cetus is Mira, though you'll be lucky to spot it. This red giant is a variable star, meaning that its brightness changes over time. It was the first variable star to be observed and measured. Astronomers in the 1600s noticed that it seemed to disappear and then reappear in a cycle lasting 330 days. They named it Mira, from the word 'miraculous'. The star doesn't actually disappear, it just gets so faint that we can no longer see it with the naked eye.

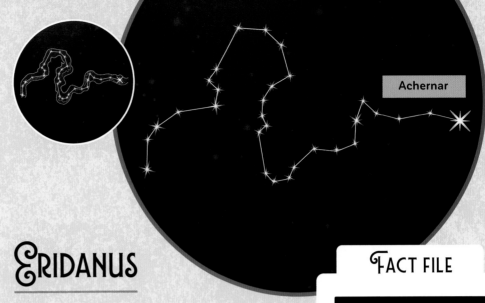

Achernar

ERIDANUS

Eridanus is a very long constellation that is meant to represent a river, as shown by a long, meandering string of stars. It might take its name from Eridu, a city in ancient Babylon. The river starts near Rigel in the constellation of Orion (see page 116), then snakes down into the southern skies until you reach its brightest star, Achernar. With a name meaning 'the river's end', Achernar is one of the brightest stars in the sky, and it is also one of the flattest. It is probably spinning extremely fast, making its equator bulge out.

FACT FILE

NAME:	Eridanus
REPRESENTS:	a river
VISIBLE:	from all of the Southern Hemisphere and the southern parts of the Northern Hemisphere
BRIGHTEST STAR:	Achernar

PISCIS AUSTRINUS

This small constellation has a name meaning 'southern fish' to distinguish it from the zodiac constellation of Pisces (see pages 104–105). Most of its stars are fairly faint, but the brightest, Fomalhaut, is very bright. You can find it by using two of the stars in the Great Square of Pegasus (see page 114), Scheat and Markab (which lie opposite Algernib and Alpheratz), as pointers. In 2008, astronomers announced that they had found what they thought was a large exoplanet orbiting Fomalhaut. However, they now think that it's most likely a cloud of dust produced from a collision between forming planets.

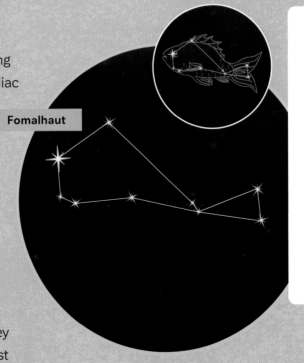

Fomalhaut

FACT FILE

NAME:	Piscis Austrinus
REPRESENTS:	a fish
VISIBLE:	from all of the Southern Hemisphere and parts of the Northern Hemisphere
BRIGHTEST STAR:	Fomalhaut

STAR CLUSTERS

Although the stars in a constellation look close together in the sky, in most cases they are actually very, very far apart in space. However, there are some groups of stars that really are close together. These are called star clusters, and they are a fascinating target for stargazing. A few can be seen with the naked eye. For others, you'll need binoculars or a telescope.

⊙ OPEN CLUSTERS

There are two types of star clusters. The first is called an open cluster, or sometimes a galactic cluster. These may have anywhere from a dozen up to a thousand or more stars. The Pleiades (see page 131) is an open cluster where you can see individual stars with the naked eye. Other clusters of this type will appear as a single dot or smudge, and you'll need a telescope to see the individual stars. The stars in these clusters are not held together in a tight shape.

An open star cluster is visible in this image of the NGC 1999 nebula.

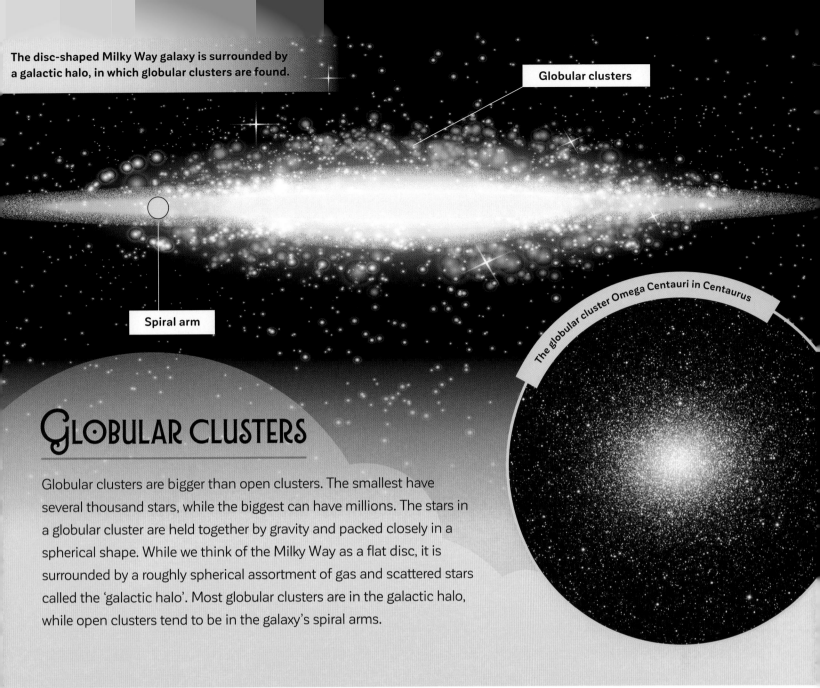

The disc-shaped Milky Way galaxy is surrounded by a galactic halo, in which globular clusters are found.

Globular clusters

Spiral arm

The globular cluster Omega Centauri in Centaurus

GLOBULAR CLUSTERS

Globular clusters are bigger than open clusters. The smallest have several thousand stars, while the biggest can have millions. The stars in a globular cluster are held together by gravity and packed closely in a spherical shape. While we think of the Milky Way as a flat disc, it is surrounded by a roughly spherical assortment of gas and scattered stars called the 'galactic halo'. Most globular clusters are in the galactic halo, while open clusters tend to be in the galaxy's spiral arms.

WHY DO CLUSTERS FORM?

The stars in both types of cluster form in clouds of gas and dust called nebulas (see pages 90–91). Globular clusters formed long ago, when there was a lot more free gas in the galaxy, which is why they contain many more stars. They contain some of the oldest stars in the galaxy, with ages of up to 13 billion years. The stars in an open cluster are younger. Although all the stars in a cluster formed around the same time, it happened much more recently than the formation of globular clusters.

OUR HOME CLUSTER

Astronomers believe that our Sun formed as part of an open cluster about 4.6 billion years ago. Once the stars had formed, the extra gas dispersed. The gravitational attraction of the remaining stars wasn't strong enough to hold them in place, so they gradually drifted apart. Now that so much time has passed, they could be anywhere in the galaxy! Astronomers look for our Sun's 'siblings' by analysing the chemicals inside distant stars. If they match the Sun's mix of chemicals, it's a good sign that they formed together with the Sun. So far, two likely candidates have been found.

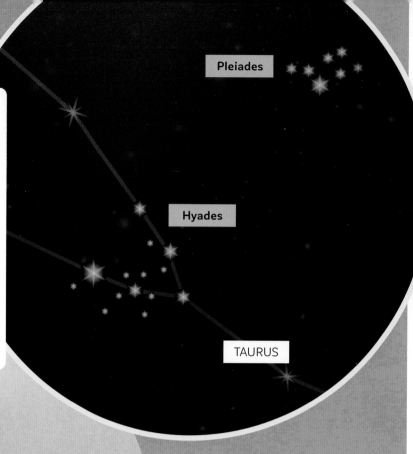

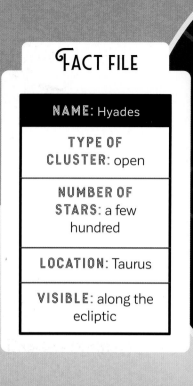

FACT FILE

NAME: Hyades
TYPE OF CLUSTER: open
NUMBER OF STARS: a few hundred
LOCATION: Taurus
VISIBLE: along the ecliptic

THE HYADES

If you look at the constellation of Taurus (see pages 98–99), you'll see a V-shaped group of stars making up the bull's face. This is actually an open cluster called the Hyades, named after five of the daughters of the Greek god Atlas. This part of the constellation is dominated by the bright-reddish star Aldebaran, but Aldebaran is not part of the cluster. It is about 65 light years away from us, while the Hyades are about 150 light years away. The five brightest stars in the Hyades have used up their hydrogen 'fuel' and are nearing the end of their lives.

THE BEEHIVE

Like many clusters, the Beehive is faint enough that you'll need really dark skies to see it at all. It will appear as a faint, fuzzy object, about three times the diameter of the Moon. Binoculars or a small telescope will let you see some of its stars, looking like a glittery swarm. This cluster is in Cancer (see page 100), but that's a faint constellation that's hard to spot. You'll have a better chance of finding the Beehive if you look for Regulus in the constellation of Leo (see page 100) and the pair of Castor and Pollux in the constellation of Gemini (see page 99). The Beehive cluster is halfway between them.

FACT FILE

NAME: Beehive or Praesepe
TYPE OF CLUSTER: open
NUMBER OF STARS: about 1,000
LOCATION: Cancer
VISIBLE: along the ecliptic

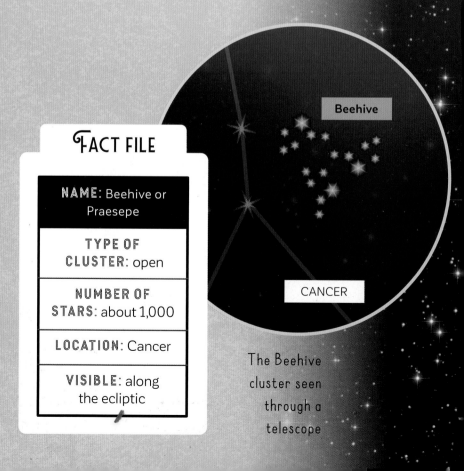

The Beehive cluster seen through a telescope

THE PLEIADES

The Pleiades may be the best-known star cluster, because you can easily see with the naked eye that it is a group of stars. It is named after seven sisters in Greek mythology, because at least seven stars can be seen easily. (At the bottom of the cluster, Merope is a bit harder to spot, and legend says that her light is dimmer because she married a mortal instead of a god.) With telescopes, astronomers have discovered that the cluster actually has more than 1,000 stars. The Pleiades lie just to the side of the horns of Taurus.

FACT FILE

NAME: Pleiades	
TYPE OF CLUSTER: open	
NUMBER OF STARS: more than 1,000	
LOCATION: Taurus	
VISIBLE: along the ecliptic	

The star clusters Hyades (left) and Pleiades (right)

WHAT'S IN A NAME?

The Beehive cluster was known to the Greeks and Romans as Praesepe, which is Latin for 'manger'. They saw two of the stars in Cancer as donkeys who were eating from it. Over the years, astronomers gave it names such as Achlus ('little mist') and Nephelion ('little cloud'). Chinese astronomers saw it as a ghost riding in a carriage, and gave it a name meaning 'piled-up corpses'. The cluster is now more commonly known as the Beehive – though no one knows why! Possibly because it looks like a cloud of bees.

Double Cluster

Based on the name, it should come as no surprise that the Double Cluster is actually not one star cluster, but two! The two clusters are about 7,500 light years away from us, but only a few hundred light years apart from each other. For us to see them at such a distance, they must contain bright stars. Although the clusters lie within the constellation of Perseus, it might be easier to use Cassiopeia to find them (see page 120). From the centre of the five stars that make up Cassiopeia, follow the line down to the star below it (on the shallower 'V' shape) and keep going along that line. Scan the sky with binoculars until you find a double cluster.

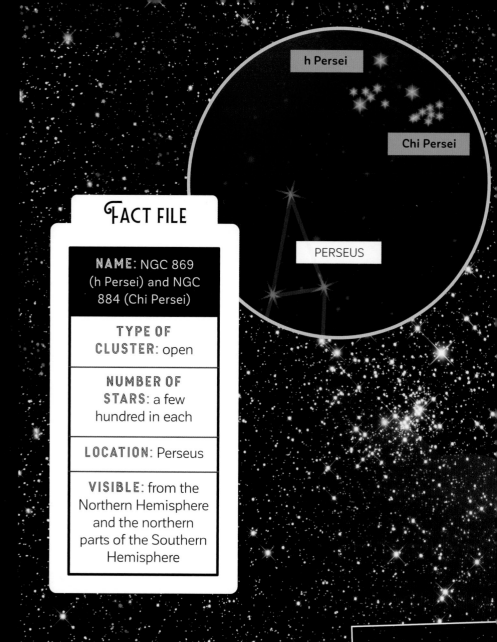

h Persei

Chi Persei

PERSEUS

FACT FILE

NAME: NGC 869 (h Persei) and NGC 884 (Chi Persei)

TYPE OF CLUSTER: open

NUMBER OF STARS: a few hundred in each

LOCATION: Perseus

VISIBLE: from the Northern Hemisphere and the northern parts of the Southern Hemisphere

Great Globular Cluster

This fabulous cluster goes by several different names, but any astronomer will recognise it as M13. It is one of the objects catalogued back in the late 1700s by Charles Messier (see pages 20–21). This huge cluster contains hundreds of thousands of stars that are almost as old as the Universe. It's in the constellation of Hercules (see page 111), but if you're having trouble finding that, look for the very bright stars Vega (in Lyra, page 112) and Arcturus (in Boötes, page 110). The square-ish Keystone shape in Hercules is about one-third of the way from Vega to Arcturus. The cluster lies between the two stars at one side of the Keystone.

FACT FILE

NAME: Hercules Globular Cluster or M13

TYPE OF CLUSTER: globular

NUMBER OF STARS: several hundred thousand

LOCATION: Hercules

VISIBLE: from the Northern Hemisphere (April–November) and the Southern Hemisphere (June–September)

The Great Globular Cluster in Hercules

The Double Cluster in Perseus

Coma Star Cluster

COMA BERENICES

COMA STAR CLUSTER

This cluster, found in a constellation called Coma Berenices (see page 46), contains just a few dozen bright stars. In really dark skies, you can see it as many faint stars clustered in a wispy group that takes up a fairly large section of the sky. Start with the backwards question mark shape that forms part of Leo (see page 100), with the very bright star Regulus at the bottom. Follow a line from Regulus back through the triangle of stars making up the lion's hindquarters, and it will lead to the Coma Star Cluster.

FACT FILE

NAME:	Coma Star Cluster
TYPE OF CLUSTER:	open
NUMBER OF STARS:	about 40
LOCATION:	Coma Berenices
VISIBLE:	from the Northern Hemisphere and most of the Southern Hemisphere

Coma Berenices is named after Queen Berenice.

M13

HERCULES

HAIR THAT'S TRULY STELLAR

Coma Berenices is the only one of the 88 constellations to be named after a real historical person. Berenice was queen of what is now Libya in the third century BCE. According to legend, she cut off her beautiful hair as an offering to the gods in return for her husband returning safely from battle. She put the clippings in a temple, but by the next morning they had disappeared. Her astronomer soon found a constellation, which he said was the missing hair – put in the stars by the gods as a reward for her sacrifice!

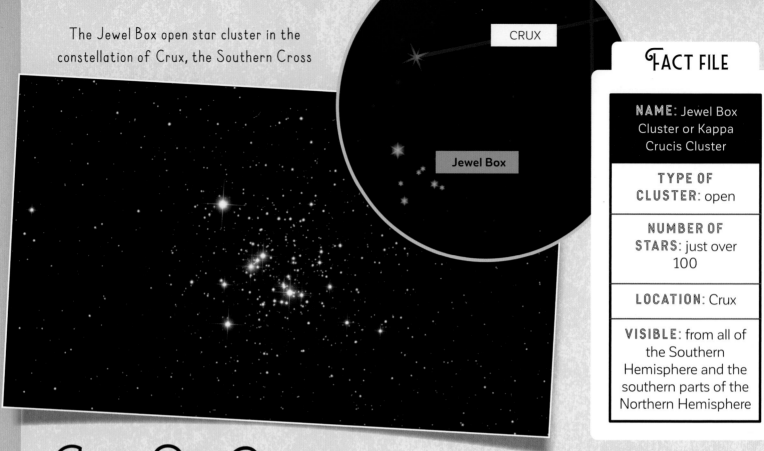

The Jewel Box open star cluster in the constellation of Crux, the Southern Cross

CRUX

Jewel Box

FACT FILE

NAME: Jewel Box Cluster or Kappa Crucis Cluster	
TYPE OF CLUSTER: open	
NUMBER OF STARS: just over 100	
LOCATION: Crux	
VISIBLE: from all of the Southern Hemisphere and the southern parts of the Northern Hemisphere	

Jewel Box Cluster

When the English astronomer John Herschel saw this beautiful open cluster through a telescope, he described it as 'a superb piece of fancy jewellery'. It's easy to find because it's very close to one of the bright stars that form the constellation Crux (see page 124). With the naked eye, it will look like a fuzzy star. With a telescope or binoculars, you can make out the pyramid shape formed by its brightest stars. The four brightest are sometimes known as the 'traffic light' because of their different colours. This is a very young cluster – only about 14 million years old.

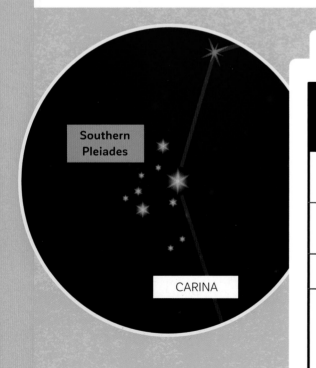

Southern Pleiades

CARINA

FACT FILE

NAME: Theta Carinae Cluster or Southern Pleiades	
TYPE OF CLUSTER: globular	
NUMBER OF STARS: about 60	
LOCATION: Carina	
VISIBLE: from all of the Southern Hemisphere and the most southern parts of the Northern Hemisphere	

Theta Carinae Cluster

This cluster includes Theta Carinae, one of the stars in the constellation of Carina (see page 125). This fairly bright star is surrounded by dozens of fainter ones that should be visible with binoculars or a telescope. This cluster is often known as the Southern Pleiades, because its stars form a shape that resembles that of the Pleiades (see page 131). In terms of distance, it is one of the closest clusters – only about 547 light years away from Earth. It covers an area of the sky nearly twice as wide as the diameter of the Moon.

Omega Centauri has a diameter of more than 150 light years.

Omega Centauri

Globular clusters are big, but the cluster called Omega Centauri is really big! Astronomers think that it is the biggest cluster in the Milky Way, with millions of stars. These stars are tightly packed, with an average distance of 0.16 light years between them. That sounds like a lot, until you consider that the Sun's nearest neighbour is 4.25 light years away – more than 26 times further! At first, the Greek astronomer Ptolemy thought Omega Centauri was a star. Once telescopes were invented, astronomers identified it as a nebula, and finally as a cluster. You can find it by looking above and to the left of the top star of the constellation Crux (see page 124).

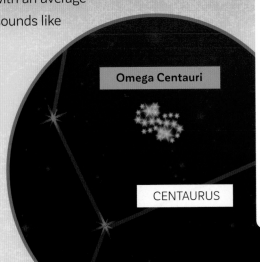

Omega Centauri

CENTAURUS

Fact File

NAME: Omega Centauri or NGC 5139
TYPE OF CLUSTER: globular
NUMBER OF STARS: about 10 million
LOCATION: Centaurus
VISIBLE: from all of the Southern Hemisphere and the southern parts of the Northern Hemisphere

A Captured Galaxy?

In addition to its huge size, Omega Centauri is unusual for another reason: its stars formed at different periods. In most other clusters, all the stars are about the same age. Astronomers think that Omega Centauri may be what's left of a dwarf galaxy that was captured by the Milky Way. All the outer stars were stripped away, leaving only the dense mass of stars at the core.

LIFE CYCLE OF A STAR

Our Sun has been shining for nearly 5 billion years, much longer than humans (or even dinosaurs!) have been around. But it won't last forever. Eventually, the hydrogen in its core will begin to run out, and the Sun will stop shining. This has already happened to billions of other stars in the Universe. But what exactly is happening, and why?

Stellar nebula

White dwarf

Average star

Planetary nebula

Massive star

Red giant

Red super giant

Supernova

The life cycle of a star

'LIVING' STARS

Stars are not alive, but we often talk about them as though they are, using words like 'born' or 'die'. This is because stars follow a regular process from when they first form to when they eventually stop shining – similar to the way that a human being is born, grows up, and finally dies. The stars in our galaxy represent all different stages of this 'life cycle'. By studying them, astronomers have worked out what happens to stars as they age.

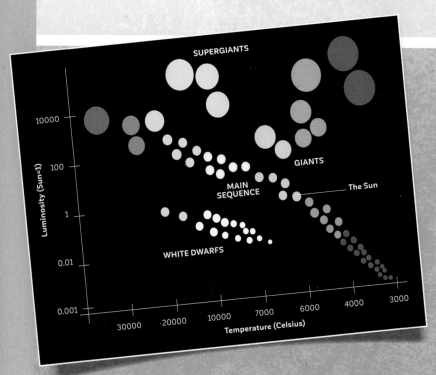

SUPERGIANTS

GIANTS

MAIN SEQUENCE

The Sun

WHITE DWARFS

Luminosity (Sun=1)

10000

100

1

0.01

0.001

30000   20000   10000   7000   6000   4000   3000

Temperature (Celsius)

This graph shows the classes of stars, their luminosity (brightness) compared to our Sun, and their temperature.

A STAR IS BORN

A star begins its life inside a nebula (see pages 90–93 and 138–139). Gas and dust clump together to form protostars that eventually become stars. Once a star has enough mass, nuclear fusion begins in its core. The star is now said to be a main sequence star. It will stay this way, shining brightly, for most of its life. Main sequence stars come in a range of sizes, colours and temperatures.

Supernova!

When a star's hydrogen runs out, nuclear fusion can no longer take place. The core contracts, while the star's outer shell expands. This shell cools and glows red, and the star is now called a red giant. (Betelgeuse is at this stage of its life cycle – see page 117.) What happens next depends on how much mass the star contains. If it is about ten times as massive as the Sun, it will eventually explode – an event called a supernova. The remains of the supernova sometimes become a super-dense star called a neutron star. If the star was really big, what's left after the explosion is swallowed by its own gravity and becomes a black hole.

Neutron star

Black hole

A Quieter End

For smaller stars, like the Sun, the end is much less spectacular. After the red giant phase, the core collapses again and becomes denser. The star's outer layers of gas are blown off, forming a cloud known as a planetary nebula. The core is now a white dwarf star, which is small but very dense. The white dwarf slowly cools until it becomes a black dwarf. These stars no longer give off heat or light – or any type of energy at all. The Universe is not yet old enough for any black dwarfs to exist – but they will eventually.

Artist's impression of a white dwarf

Artist's impression of a supernova remnant

NEBULAS

Nebulas are beautiful objects, making an exciting target for a stargazer. Thanks to modern telescopes, which can see far into deep space (and also 'see' using different types of energy – see pages 24–27), we have discovered some truly amazing sights. Simply put, a nebula is a cloud of gas and dust in space. But within that definition there is a huge amount of variation!

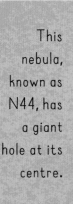

This nebula, known as N44, has a giant hole at its centre.

WHERE DO NEBULAS COME FROM?

You've probably heard it said that space is a vacuum, but this isn't strictly true. Something called the interstellar medium (ISM) exists in the vast emptiness of space. The ISM is 99 per cent gas (hydrogen and helium) with a little bit of dust. The atoms of gas and dust are incredibly thinly spread, but the huge distances between the stars mean that the matter adds up enough for gravity to sometimes start pulling it together into nebulas. Nebulas are often huge – up to hundreds of light years in diameter – but they are only fractionally denser than the space surrounding them. In fact, most nebulas are less dense than any 'vacuum' we've been able to create on Earth!

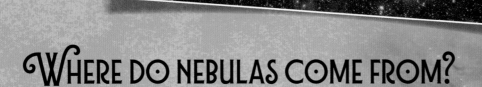

TYPES OF NEBULAS

Nebulas come in different types. The most common type is the diffuse nebula, which spreads out with no defined boundaries or regular shape. Diffuse nebulas are often divided into emission nebulas, which emit energy, and reflection nebulas, which don't emit their own radiation, but instead reflect light from a nearby star. There are also dark nebulas, which are clouds of dust that block the light from objects behind them. Planetary nebulas are shells of gas produced by a dying star (see page 137). The last type of nebula is a supernova remnant, which remains after a massive star explodes.

Dark nebula known as the Horsehead Nebula

Emission nebula

Reflection nebula

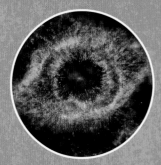

Planetary nebula

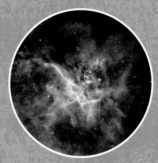

Supernova remnant

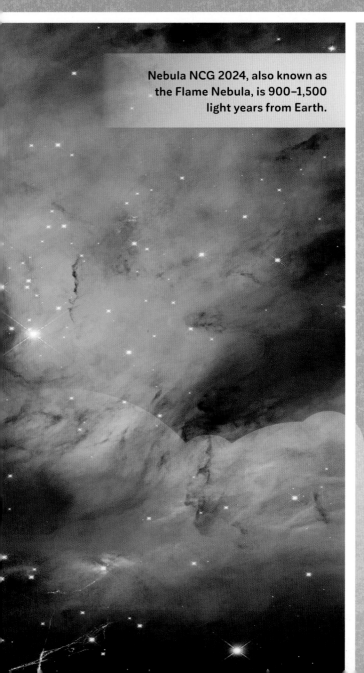

Nebula NCG 2024, also known as the Flame Nebula, is 900–1,500 light years from Earth.

NAMING NEBULAS

All nebulas have an official name made up of letters and numbers. But many nebulas also have another name that is more commonly used, especially by amateur stargazers. These names are often based on the shape of the nebula. There is a Horsehead Nebula and a Jellyfish Nebula and a Spaghetti Nebula, which looks like a plate of pasta. You can probably guess what the Soap Bubble Nebula and Lemon Slice Nebula look like! There is even a Pac-Man Nebula, which looks like a character from an old video game.

The Pac-Man Nebula

CRAB NEBULA

There's a lot that's special about the Crab Nebula. It was the first object to be added to the Messier catalogue (see pages 20–21), so it's also known as M1. What's more, it's the remains of a supernova explosion that humans actually witnessed! On 4 July 1054 CE, Chinese astronomers noticed what they called a 'guest star' in the constellation of Taurus. This new star was brighter than Venus, and it lasted for about two years before fading from view. Using telescopes, astronomers in the 1800s observed a fuzzy patch that was shaped a bit like a crab, but no one realised it was the same thing as the 'guest star' until much later.

ORION NEBULA

If you look at the constellation of Orion (see pages 116–117), you'll see a line of fainter stars hanging down from the belt. These represent the hunter's sword. Halfway along it is a fuzzy patch that isn't a star at all – it's a beautiful nebula that you can actually see with the naked eye. Telescopes such as Hubble have provided incredible views of its clouds. Inside the nebula, maybe as many as a thousand stars are being born. In fact, astronomers can see an open cluster of young stars within the nebula. The four brightest stars within the nebula form a group known as the Trapezium because of its geometric shape.

The nebula within the constellation of Orion

NAME: Crab Nebula or M1

TYPE OF NEBULA: supernova remnant

DISTANCE FROM EARTH: 6,500 light years

LOCATION: Taurus

The Crab Nebula is a supernova remnant.

RING NEBULA

The Ring Nebula is a popular target for amateur astronomers. Seen through a small telescope, it looks like a pale ring of white smoke. Unlike the Crab Nebula, this cloud didn't form in an explosion. It is the outer shell of a dying red giant star that was ejected into space. The core of the star remains as a white dwarf at the centre of the nebula, but it gives off so little light that it's difficult to see. The nebula is expanding at a rate of about 19 km (12 miles) per second. This has been going on for at least 1,000 years, and will continue for about 10,000 more.

FACT FILE

NAME: Ring Nebula or M57

TYPE OF NEBULA: planetary	DISTANCE FROM EARTH: 2,000 light years
LOCATION: Lyra	

The Ring Nebula in a composite image with visible light and infrared

FACT FILE

NAME: Orion Nebula or M42

TYPE OF NEBULA: diffuse (emission/ reflection)	DISTANCE FROM EARTH: 1,344 light years
	LOCATION: Orion

GETTING A BETTER VIEW

You may be lucky enough to see a nebula through an amateur telescope, but these telescopes only take in visible light. To get a clearer picture of what nebulas are actually like, astronomers use other types of telescopes, which sense different kinds of energy. An infrared telescope can sense the heat of stars whose light is blocked by the dust. Radio and X-ray telescopes also provide useful information. Many of the spectacular nebula photos that you see on these pages are composite images, made from data from two or more types of telescope.

The Cat's Eye Nebula as seen by the Hubble Space Telescope

CAT'S EYE NEBULA

The Cat's Eye Nebula was one of the first planetary nebulas to be discovered. In fact, it is the reason that planetary nebulas got their name. When the astronomer William Herschel first saw it in 1786 through his relatively small telescope, he was struck by its shape. It reminded him of the planet Uranus. So this type of object is still called a planetary nebula, even though it has nothing to do with planets! The Cat's Eye Nebula is made up of the gassy outer shell of a dying star. Its complex structure has been imaged by all types of telescopes, from infrared to X-ray.

EAGLE NEBULA

The Eagle Nebula is one of the Milky Way's most spectacular sights, but only a large telescope will show it in all its glory. Astronomers have been putting it in their catalogues since the 1700s, but it's only more recently – thanks to improved technology – that astronomers have been able to study it in detail. The Eagle Nebula includes several regions where stars are forming, including the 'Pillars of Creation', which were made famous by a stunning image taken in 1995 by the Hubble Space Telescope (see pages 26–27). Another star-forming area, the Stellar Spire, is a whopping 9.5 light years tall! You can find the nebula by looking for the 'teapot' in Sagittarius (see pages 102–103), then following the line of the side with the spout upwards.

The Eagle Nebula with the 'Pillars of Creation'

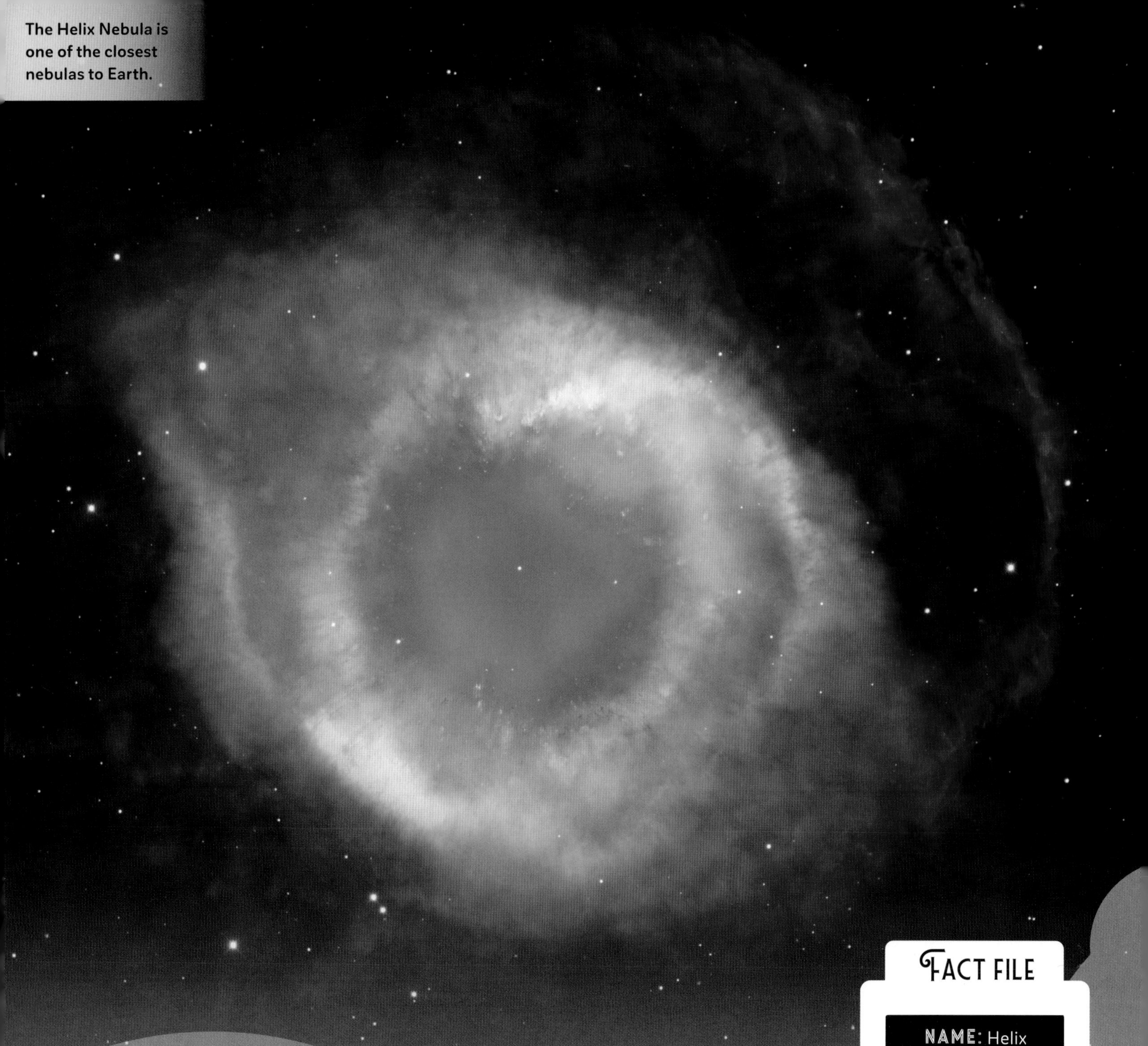

The Helix Nebula is one of the closest nebulas to Earth.

Helix Nebula

Its double-ring structure gives the Helix Nebula its name, but if you look at the stunning images taken by infrared and visible light telescopes, you'll see why some people call it the Eye of God Nebula. It's like a massive eye – one that is nearly 6 light years wide – looking down at you from the depths of space! If you can find the bright star Fomalhaut (see page 127), use your outstretched hand to measure about 10 degrees to the northwest (see pages 44–45). With binoculars, it will look like a grey circle about the size of the Moon. With a small telescope you may be able to see its ring shape.

Fact File

NAME: Helix Nebula or Eye of God Nebula

TYPE OF NEBULA: planetary

DISTANCE FROM EARTH: 650 light years

LOCATION: Aquarius

The Lagoon Nebula, where bright
new stars are forming

LAGOON NEBULA

You can navigate to the Lagoon Nebula by using the 'teapot' of Sagittarius (see pages 102–103). Compared to the Eagle Nebula (see page 142), the Lagoon Nebula is closer to the spout and off to the right a bit. It's no coincidence that these two nebulas are in a similar location: Sagittarius lies along the arcing disc of the Milky Way, so it's full of deep-sky objects. The Lagoon Nebula will look like a faint patch, about three times as wide as a full Moon.

The Carina Nebula

CARINA NEBULA

The gorgeous (and enormous) Carina Nebula is four times the size of the Orion Nebula, but it's really only visible from the Southern Hemisphere. It contains several different regions where stars are being born, while at its centre is a huge dying star. This star, called Eta Carinae, is a poster child for the motto 'live fast and die young'. It's nearly 150 times as massive as the Sun, but only 2–3 million years old. Since the early 1800s, it has gone through periods where it became one of the brightest stars in the sky. But Eta Carinae is losing mass quickly and will end up exploding in a supernova.

BLOCKING THE VIEW

Nebulas are gorgeous to look at, but they sometimes get in the way. Take the Pistol Star, for example. This enormous star is about 10 million times as bright as the Sun. Even from a distance of 25,000 light years, you'd assume a star that bright would be easy to spot. But the Pistol Star was only discovered in the 1990s. Thanks to the clouds of dust in the way, we can't see it at all! It took Hubble's infrared capabilities to sense its heat.

TARANTULA NEBULA

The Tarantula Nebula is both very big and very bright. Luckily, it is also very, very far away. It's so far away that it's not even part of the Milky Way! It's located in the Large Magellanic Cloud (see pages 150–151), which is a small galaxy that orbits the Milky Way. If the Tarantula Nebula were as close to Earth as the Orion Nebula is, it would be so bright in the night sky that its light would cast shadows on the ground! This nebula got its name from its glowing filaments of dust, which look like a tarantula's legs. Inside the nebula, hundreds of thousands of stars are forming.

FACT FILE

NAME: Tarantula Nebula

TYPE OF NEBULA: diffuse (emission)

DISTANCE FROM EARTH: 160,000 light years

LOCATION: Dorado

The centre of the Tarantula Nebula

DISTANT GALAXIES

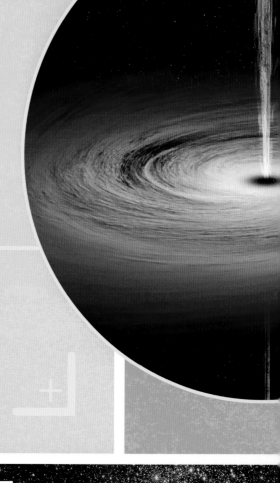

The Milky Way is full of wonders, such as giant stars and beautiful nebulas. For a long time, humans thought that the Universe extended no further beyond it – that what we could see was all that there was. We now know that there are billions of other galaxies in the Universe. And you can see some of them from Earth!

GALAXY SHAPES

Galaxies come in different shapes and sizes. The smallest dwarf galaxies may have as few as 100 million stars, while the biggest galaxies have over a trillion. The most common galaxy shape is a flat disc in a spiral shape, like the Milky Way. More than half of spiral galaxies have a barred shape running through the centre. In an elliptical galaxy, the stars are arranged in a shape that ranges from nearly spherical to more like a rugby ball. Only a small percentage of galaxies are irregular, with no recognisable shape.

Irregular

Barred spiral

Artist's impression of a black hole pulling in matter from a nearby star

Black Holes

Just like the Milky Way, nearly all large galaxies have a supermassive black hole at the centre. There are also smaller black holes sprinkled throughout the Universe. The gravity of a black hole is so strong that nothing can escape, not even light. This makes them very hard to study! It was only in the 2010s that astronomers found solid evidence of the Milky Way's black hole. To find a black hole, you can't look for the hole itself – you have to look for its effects on nearby matter.

Where Are We?

We know where our Solar System sits in relation to the rest of the Milky Way. It's a lot harder, though, to know where the Milky Way is located in relation to the rest of the Universe. The Universe is simply too big, and its parts are too similar for us to really know where its centre is, or if it has one at all. What astronomers do know is that the Milky Way is part of a cluster of galaxies called the Local Group. This is located near the edge of a bigger cluster of galaxies called the Virgo Supercluster.

Elliptical

Spiral

Wanda Díaz-Merced

Wanda Díaz-Merced began to lose her sight as a teenager. Despite her disability, she was determined to keep studying and pursue a career. One day, a friend played her an audio recording of a burst of energy from the Sun. Díaz-Merced was fascinated by the idea of using sound to study space. She programmed software to turn astronomical data into sound, and she used it to help identify black holes in galaxies. It turned out that using sound mixed with visible information gave the best results!

BORN: 1982, Puerto Rico, USA

The Andromeda Galaxy

If you're going to explore the Universe's other galaxies, the Andromeda Galaxy is a good place to start. It's not our nearest neighbour in space, but it was the first galaxy outside the Milky Way to be discovered. Even better, it's fairly easy to spot!

The Andromeda Galaxy

What is it?

Persian astronomers, working in the days before telescopes, saw Andromeda as a cloudy smear. When Charles Messier (see pages 20–21) put Andromeda in his catalogue as M31, he called it a nebula. In 1850, William Parsons saw its spiral structure, but astronomers still thought that Andromeda was a nebula within the Milky Way. It wasn't until the 1920s that Edwin Hubble, using a technique developed by Henrietta Swan Leavitt (see page 121), proved that Andromeda was a separate galaxy.

CASSIOPEIA

Andromeda Galaxy (M31)

ANDROMEDA

Location of the Andromeda Galaxy

Finding Andromeda

The Andromeda Galaxy is 2.5 million light years away, making it the most distant object that you can see with the naked eye. It gets its name because it lies within the constellation of Andromeda (see page 114), and in dark skies it will look like a small, elongated smudge. Because the constellation of Andromeda is not particularly bright, many people use Cassiopeia (see pages 120–121) to point the way instead. Find Schedar, the brightest star in the constellation, located at the tip of the deeper 'V' shape. That 'V' shape points almost directly to Andromeda. It's easier to spot using averted vision – looking at it out of the corner of your eye – as this uses the part of your eye that is most sensitive to light.

Galaxies Collide

Galaxies are always on the move. As the Universe expands, galaxies move outwards with it, like dots drawn on the outside of a balloon that is then blown up. But within a cluster of galaxies, gravity can pull them towards each other. And sometimes, they collide! Andromeda is moving towards the Milky Way at 110 km (70 miles) per second, and in about 4 billion years, the two galaxies will collide and merge.

The colliding galaxies NGC 2207 and IC 2163, as seen by the Hubble Space Telescope

LOOKING BACK IN TIME

The Universe is so big that looking into its depths is taking a trip back in time. Light travels incredibly fast, but to cover the vast distances of space takes a very, very long time. In 2020, astronomers spotted a galaxy about 13.4 billion light years away. That means that the light picked up by their telescopes left the galaxy 13.4 billion years ago. Who knows what has happened to its stars in the time since then? The age of the Universe is thought to be about 13.8 billion years, so we are seeing the Universe as it was when it was just 400 million years old.

GN-z11 is the farthest galaxy yet discovered. It is 13.4 billion light years away.

FACT FILE

NAME: Large Magellanic Cloud

TYPE OF GALAXY: spiral

DISTANCE FROM EARTH: 160,000 light years

LOCATION: on the border between Mensa and Dorado

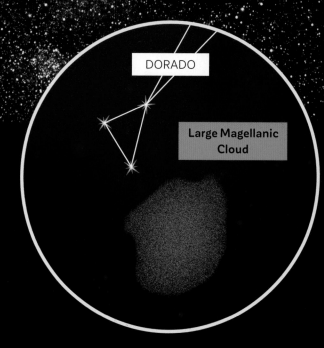

DORADO

Large Magellanic Cloud

LARGE MAGELLANIC CLOUD

The Large Magellanic Cloud is what's called a satellite galaxy. It is affected by the gravity of its larger neighbour, the Milky Way, and travels through space alongside it – a bit like the way that Earth and the other planets are bound by the Sun's gravity. The Large Magellanic Cloud is much smaller than the Milky Way, with only a few billion stars. In the sky, it looks like a dusty patch. The area where it is found, between the constellations Mensa and Dorado (see page 47), is a fairly dark region of the sky, which makes the galaxy easier to see. You can use the two brightest stars, Sirius (in Canis Major, pages 118–119) and Canopus (in Carina, page 125), to find it. Follow a line from Sirius to Canopus, passing to the right-hand side of Canopus, and that will lead you to the Large Magellanic Cloud.

SMALL MAGELLANIC CLOUD

The Small Magellanic Cloud is another satellite galaxy that's also visible with the naked eye from the Southern Hemisphere. The two Magellanic Clouds orbit each other – this takes about 900 million years – as they travel in orbit around the Milky Way. The Small Magellanic Cloud contains only a few hundred million stars, but because it is so close to us, it takes up about the same amount of sky as ten full Moons. Astronomers think that the Small Magellanic Cloud was once a barred spiral galaxy, but that the Milky Way's gravity has distorted its shape.

The Small Magellanic Cloud

FACT FILE

NAME: Small Magellanic Cloud	
TYPE OF GALAXY: irregular	DISTANCE FROM EARTH: 200,000 light years
LOCATION: on the border between Tucana and Hydrus	

LEGENDS ABOUT THE CLOUDS

Because they are only visible from the Southern Hemisphere and the lands around the Equator, the Magellanic clouds don't feature in the legends of Northern Hemisphere civilisations. They take their current names from the Portuguese explorer Ferdinand Magellan, who wrote about seeing the Large Magellanic Cloud in 1519, while leading the first voyage to sail all the way around the world. But at that point the clouds had already been a familiar sight for Australia's aboriginal peoples for thousands of years. To them, the galaxies were the camping places of an old man and woman who were known as the Jukara.

Portuguese explorer Ferdinand Magellan

Whirlpool Galaxy

Have you ever sat in the bath and watched the water spiral down the plughole? Imagine that shape, but scaled up to galactic proportions, and you'll get the beautiful spiral of the aptly named Whirlpool Galaxy. In the arms, clusters of new stars are being formed. There is a small companion galaxy at the end of one of the arms. To stargazers on Earth, the galaxy appears face-on, giving a fantastic view of its spiral shape. Best of all, it's fairly easy to find! Simply look for the Plough asterism (see pages 97 and 108–109) and find the star at the end of the handle. Look down from that, about 3.5 degrees.

URSA MAJOR

Whirlpool Galaxy

FACT FILE

NAME: Whirlpool Galaxy or M51	
TYPE OF GALAXY: spiral	DISTANCE FROM EARTH: 31 million light years
LOCATION: Canes Venatici	

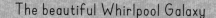

The beautiful Whirlpool Galaxy

VIRGO

Sombrero Galaxy

Spica

CORVUS

GRAND DESIGNS

The Whirlpool Galaxy is classed as a 'grand-design' spiral galaxy because the shape of its two curving arms is so clear and well-defined. They curve outward from the galaxy's central bulge. Some spiral galaxies, such as the Large Magellanic Cloud, have only one arm. There is evidence that the Milky Way has four. Some galaxies have arms that are very tightly curled, while others have much looser arms. The two arms of the Whirlpool Galaxy, with their graceful curves, seem almost perfect.

CIGAR GALAXY

For a long time, astronomers thought that the Cigar Galaxy – named for its long, thin shape – was an irregular galaxy. But by using infrared, they've been able to find two spiral arms. From our perspective, the galaxy is side-on, making its structure hard to see. It is what's known as a 'starburst' galaxy, because stars are forming there at a tremendous rate – ten times faster than in the Milky Way! The Cigar Galaxy is locked in a gravitational tug-of-war with its nearest neighbour, M81 (also known as Bode's Galaxy). The turbulent conditions have created star-forming regions and make the galaxy 'glow' with X-rays.

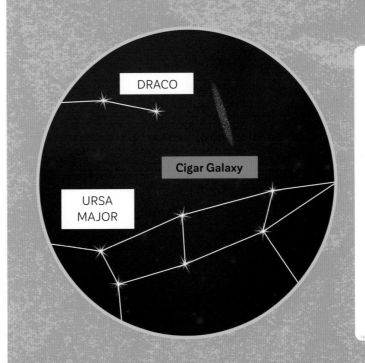

DRACO

Cigar Galaxy

URSA MAJOR

FACT FILE

NAME: Cigar Galaxy or M82

TYPE OF GALAXY: spiral

DISTANCE FROM EARTH: 12 million light years

LOCATION: Ursa Major

FACT FILE

NAME: Sombrero Galaxy or M104

TYPE OF GALAXY: spiral

DISTANCE FROM EARTH: 28 million light years

LOCATION: on the border between Virgo and Corvus

SOMBRERO GALAXY

You'll need a telescope to spot the Sombrero Galaxy, named for its resemblance to a Mexican hat. It has a large, bright central bulge surrounded by a dusty outer disc that appears virtually edge-on to viewers on Earth. With a mass of about 800 billion times that of our Sun, the Sombrero Galaxy is one of the most massive objects in the Virgo galaxy cluster. Because it's fairly faint, it's not the easiest galaxy to find, but you can star-hop to it using the bright star Spica in the constellation of Virgo (see page 101). Below and to the right are the four stars making up the constellation of Corvus, or 'The Crow'. There is a chain of faint stars extending upwards, leading to the Sombrero Galaxy.

The Sombrero Galaxy, M104

SEEING THE STARS

Are dark skies rare where you live? You can still see a multitude of stars by visiting a planetarium. These are like theatres where the domed ceiling becomes the celestial sphere. They put on shows demonstrating how to star-hop around the constellations, or films about space. At space museums, you can walk around fascinating exhibits on all aspects of space exploration, and some large observatories are also open to visitors, although usually only professional astronomers are allowed to use their telescopes.

The tilted dome of a planetarium gives the audience the sensation that they are immersed in the Universe.

PLACES TO VISIT

AUSTRALIA

Arkaroola Astronomical Observatory
2948 Arkaroola Road 5701, Arkaroola Village, Australia
www.arkaroola.com.au/astronomy-tours
At this privately owned observatory, you can take part in stargazing evenings under some of the Southern Hemisphere's clearest skies.

Melbourne Planetarium
2 Booker Street, Spotswood, VIC 3015, Australia
museumsvictoria.com.au/scienceworks/visiting/melbourne-planetarium
This modern planetarium hosts films and star shows, and even offers school groups the opportunity to bring their sleeping bags and stay the night!

Parkes Observatory
585 Telescope Road, Parkes NSW 2870, Australia
www.parkes.atnf.csiro.au
Known affectionately as 'the Dish', this huge radio telescope played a key role in the Apollo 11 Moon landings.

Sydney Observatory
1003 Upper Fort Street, Millers Point NSW 2000, Australia
www.maas.museum/sydney-observatory
At this historic site, teams of female 'human computers' measured the position of over 430,000 stars – a project that took nearly a century.

CANADA

ASTROLab at Mont-Megantic National Park
189, route du Parc, Notre-Dame-des-Bois, Québec, Canada J0B 2E0
www.astrolab.qc.ca/en/
You can tour this observatory during the day, and a few nights a year they open their telescopes up to the public!

Ontario Science Centre
770 Don Mills Road, Toronto, Canada M3C 1T3
www.ontariosciencecentre.ca
At this science museum's planetarium, sit back and enjoy an amazing virtual journey through the Solar System and beyond.

Rothney Astrophysical Observatory
210 Avenue W, Hwy 22 S, Foothills No. 31, AB T0L 1W0 Canada
science.ucalgary.ca/rothney-observatory
Researchers explore the skies at this scientific observatory, which also offers tours and stargazing events.

GERMANY

ESO Supernova Planetarium
Karl-Schwarzschild-Strasse 2, Garching bei München, Germany
supernova.eso.org
This astronomy centre is located at the site of the European Southern Observatory headquarters. There are exhibitions, guided tours and planetarium shows.

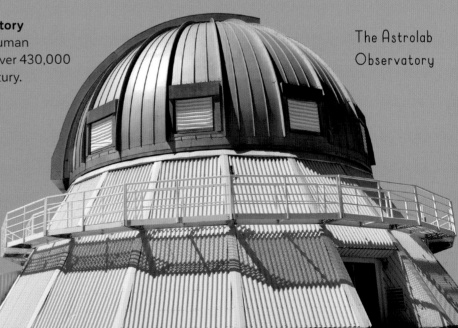

The Astrolab Observatory

NEW ZEALAND

Stardome Observatory
670 Manukau Road, Epsom, Auckland 1345, New Zealand
www.stardome.org.nz
Visitors to New Zealand's first and largest planetarium can enjoy a gallery of exhibits about space as well as shows in the state-of-the art theatre.

SOUTH AFRICA

South African Astronomical Observatory
Old Fraserburg Road, Sutherland 6920, South Africa
www.saao.ac.za
Located north-east of Cape Town, this observatory has several impressive telescopes. You can tour them by night to take advantage of the perfect dark-sky conditions.

SPAIN

L'Hemisfèric
Avenida Professor López Piñero 7, 46013 Valencia, Spain
www.cac.es/en/hemisferic
This high-tech planetarium is housed in a stunning building more than 100 metres (330 feet) long.

UK

Glasgow Science Centre Planetarium
50 Pacific Quay, Glasgow G51 1EA, Scotland
www.glasgowsciencecentre.org
Part of a wide-ranging science centre, the Glasgow Planetarium hosts immersive digital shows where visitors can go on a virtual tour of the Solar System.

Jodrell Bank
Macclesfield, Cheshire SK11 9DL, England
www.jodrellbank.net
This historic site includes the iconic Lovell Telescope, the world's third-largest steerable radio telescope. It collects radio waves from the depths of space.

National Space Centre
Exploration Drive, Leicester LE4 5NS, England
www.spacecentre.co.uk
This fascinating museum hosts hands-on exhibits about space travel, the Solar System and beyond, as well as the UK's largest planetarium.

Royal Observatory, Greenwich
Blackheath Avenue, London SE10 8XJ, England
www.rmg.co.uk/royal-observatory
This building sits astride the Prime Meridian, marking 0 degrees longitude. There are historic telescopes on display, and a new digital planetarium is nearby.

USA

Adler Planetarium
1300 South Lake Shore Drive, Chicago, IL 60605
www.adlerplanetarium.org
Located on the shores of Lake Michigan, this large planetarium has displays about space and interactive star shows.

The Lovell Telescope

Burke Baker Planetarium

5555 Hermann Park Drive, Houston, TX 77030
www.hmns.org/planetarium
The domed theatre at this planetarium has one of the world's most advanced simulators, allowing viewers to enjoy stunning star shows and films about space.

Griffith Observatory

2800 East Observatory Road, Los Angeles, CA 90027
www.griffithobservatory.org
This iconic building, which has featured in films and TV shows, includes a planetarium, an observatory, and exhibits about space.

Hayden Planetarium

200 Central Park West, New York, NY 10024
www.amnh.org/research/hayden-planetarium
Part of the American Museum of Natural History, this stunning planetarium is a 26.5-metre (87-foot) diameter sphere that sits inside a transparent glass cube.

Kitt Peak National Observatory

950 North Cherry Avenue, Tucson, AZ 85719
www.noao.edu/kpno
The clear Arizona skies are great for stargazing, and Kitt Peak houses a diverse collection of research telescopes, nearly two dozen of which are in regular use.

Lowell Observatory

1400 West Mars Hill Road, Flagstaff, AZ 86001
www.lowell.edu
Clyde Tombaugh was working at Lowell Observatory in 1930 when he discovered Pluto. You can see his telescope, along with others.

Mauna Kea Observatories

Mauna Kea Access Road, Hilo, HI 96720
www.maunakeaobservatories.org
Only professional astronomers are allowed into the telescopes at the summit (see page 23), but visitors can enjoy stargazing and exhibits at the visitor centre.

Morrison Planetarium

55 Music Concourse Drive, San Francisco, CA 94118
www.calacademy.org/exhibits/morrison-planetarium
Located in Golden Gate Park, this planetarium boasts a 23-metre (75-foot) dome made from recycled steel.

Mount Wilson Observatory

P.O. Box 94146, Pasadena, CA 01109
www.mtwilson.edu
Mount Wilson is home of the 2.5-metre (100-inch) Hooker telescope, which was the world's largest telescope for several decades. Edwin Hubble used it to observe the Andromeda Galaxy (see pages 22–23).

National Air and Space Museum

600 Independence Avenue SW, Washington, DC 20560
www.airandspace.si.edu
This fantastic museum has a range of exhibits about flight, space exploration and astronomy, including the back-up mirror for the Hubble Space Telescope.

Palomar Observatory

35899 Canfield Road, Palomar Mountain, CA 92060
sites.astro.caltech.edu/palomar.homepage.html
On a mountaintop north of San Diego, this observatory houses the Hale Telescope, a 5-metre (200-inch) reflector that was built in 1949 and is still going strong (see page 22).

Yerkes Observatory

373 West Geneva Street, Williams Bay, WI 53191
www.yerkesobservatory.org
Built in the late 1800s, this observatory housed what was once the world's largest refracting telescope and was the site of many important discoveries (see page 22).

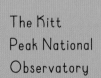

The Kitt Peak National Observatory

GLOSSARY

apparent magnitude A measure of how bright a star or other object appears, as viewed from Earth.

asterism A group of stars that appears to form a shape when viewed from Earth, but is not one of the 88 constellations.

asteroid A small, rocky object orbiting the Sun.

asteroid belt A region of space between the orbits of Mars and Jupiter in which many asteroids are found.

atmosphere A layer of gas trapped by gravity around the surface of a planet, moon or other object.

azimuth The direction of a space object from an observer, measured in degrees from the north or south point of the horizon.

binary star Two stars orbiting each other.

black hole An object in space whose gravitational pull is so strong that nothing, not even light, can escape it.

celestial sphere An imaginary sphere with an observer at its centre, on whose surface objects in space are considered to lie.

comet A rocky, icy object that travels in a long, looping path around the Sun, and which may form a long tail of gas and dust.

constellation One of the 88 agreed groups of stars that appear to form a pattern or picture when seen from Earth.

core The centre of a planet, moon or some asteroids.

crater A circular hole made when a comet, asteroid or meteorite hits another object in space.

crust The rocky outer shell of some planets, moons and asteroids.

dwarf planet A spherical object that orbits the Sun but is not massive enough to clear other objects from its orbital path.

eclipse The temporary blocking from view of the Sun, Moon or other object, when another object travels between it and Earth.

ecliptic A circle on the celestial sphere that represents the Sun's apparent path during the year.

equator An imaginary line around the middle of a planet, star or other object, like a belt.

exoplanet A planet that orbits a star other than our Sun.

fusion A nuclear reaction in which atoms fuse together in a process that releases energy.

galaxy A collection of billions of stars held together by gravity.

gravity A force that pulls objects together. The more massive an object is, the stronger its gravitational pull.

horizon The place in the distance where the sky meets the land, from the point of view of an observer.

infrared A type of electromagnetic radiation with a wavelength greater than that of visible light; it is often felt as heat.

Kuiper Belt A region of rocky, icy objects located beyond the orbit of Neptune.

light year A measure of the distance that light travels in a year, equal to about 9.5 trillion kilometres (5.9 trillion miles).

main sequence star A star in the main energy-producing stage of its evolution.

mantle A layer of hot rock found between the core and crust of some planets and other space objects.

meteor A body of matter from outer space that enters Earth's atmosphere and appears as a streak of light.

Milky Way The galaxy in which our Solar System is located.

moon An object that orbits a planet or asteroid.

nebula A cloud of dust and gas in space that is often the site of new stars being formed.

nuclear reaction A process in which the nucleus of an atom is changed by being split, or joined to another nucleus.

nucleus A rocky, icy lump that forms the main part of a comet.

Oort Cloud A spherical cloud of rocky, icy bodies at the edge of the Solar System; it is the source of many comets.

orbit The path an object takes around a larger object.

phases The different shapes that the Moon takes, as seen from Earth, as a result of its position relative to the Sun and Earth.

radar A tool that uses radio waves to find or map objects.

radio telescope A telescope that detects radio waves.

red giant A very large star in the later stages of its evolution.

reflecting telescope A type of telescope that uses a mirror to reflect the image into an eyepiece.

refracting telescope A type of telescope that takes in light through a lens and projects the image into an eyepiece.

Solar System The Sun and all the objects, including planets, asteroids and comets, that are held in place by its gravity.

spectrograph A scientific tool for measuring the light coming from an object in order to work out which elements it is made up of.

star cluster A small group of stars held together by gravity.

supernova The massive explosion that takes place when a large star reaches the end of its life cycle.

transit The passing of one object across the face of a larger one, as seen from Earth.

white dwarf A very small, dense star that forms in the late stages of the evolution of some stars.

X-ray Electromagnetic radiation with a very short wavelength.

zenith The point in the sky or celestial sphere that is directly above the observer.

zodiac A belt of the sky that follows the ecliptic and includes all visible positions of the Sun, Moon and planets.

INDEX

ACKNOWLEDGEMENTS

The publishers would like to thank the following sources for their kind permission to reproduce the pictures in this book. The page numbers for each of the photographs are listed below, giving the page on which they appear in the book and any location indicator (c-centre, t-top, b-bottom, l-left, r-right).

CREDITS

Images Shutterstock unless otherwise stated. Front Cover: Macrovector, Back Cover: br MightyRabittCrew, bl NASA, cl Makarov Konstantin, tl Stock-Asso, 6-7 Denis Belitsky, 7l Pike-28, 7r Celig, 8-9 nienora, 9tr Marzolino, 9bl Stephen Barnes, 9b Romolo Tavani, 10cr Stig Alenas, 10bl HansFree, 11t vchal, 11b Vladimir Breytberg, 12t anatoliy_gleb, 12b Captain Planet, 13t delcarmat, 13b yienkeat, 14t Jason Benz Bennee, 14b NASA, ESA, AURA/Caltech, Palomar Observatory, 15l John_Mic, 15r 963 Creation, 16cr Pam Walker, 16b Nejron Photo, 17t Savvapanf Photo, 17cr CarlsPix, 17bc Sergey Melnikov, 17bl ANGHI, 18t Pieter Kuiper/Creative Commons, 18bl spatuletail, 18br Oleg Golovnev, 19l NASA, 19tr Procy, 20t Grebenkov/Creative Commons, 20: 1. NASA/CXC/SAO; Optical: Adam Block/Mount Lemmon SkyCenter/University of Arizona, 2. NASA/JPL-Caltech/Harvard-Smithsonian CfA, 3. ESA/Hubble & NASA, V. Rubin et al., 4. NASA/CXC/CfA/R. Tuellmann et al.; Optical: NASA/AURA/STScI/J. Schmidt, 5. ESA/Hubble & NASA, F. Ferraro et al., 6. NASA/JPL-Caltech, 21t NASA, 21c Bernd Scwabe/Creative Commons, 21b Luis Alberto Canizares, 22 Noah Sauve, 23tr Johan Hagemeyer, 23b Lopolo, 24t Roger W Haworth/Creative Commons, 24c Jarek Tuszyński/CC-BY-SA-3.0 & GDFL, 24br Saber1ta983/Creative Commons, 25t Grote Reber, 25bl Carla Thomas/NASA, 25br NASA/Jim Ross, 26l NASA, 26-27 NASA, Jeff Hester, and Paul Scowen (Arizona State University), 27c NASA/JPL-Caltech, 27r NASA/CXC/NGST, 28-29 NASA, 29t Brian Donovan, 30t Marti Bug Catcher, 30-31b NicoElNino, 31t Nasky, 31br sozon, 32-33b paulista, 33t Bogdan Steblyanko, 33cr Miglena Pencheva, 34b Alexandru V, 35t Ivan Kurmyshov, 36-37 blackzheep, 37t AstroStar, 38-39 Dominik Michalek, 39t Jazziel, 40-41t Taiga, 40-41c Gubin Yury, 40-41b Brian Donovan, 42b Christian Badescu, 43t ValentinaKru, 44b stockshoppe, 44-45t Claudio Caridi, 47t H. Raab/Creative Commons, 48-49 David (Deddy) Dayag/Creative Commons, 49t AstroStar, 50cr NASA/VAULT, 50br Smithsonian Institution @ Flickr Commons, 51t NASA, 51b NASA/Aubrey Gemignani, 52t carlinjack1, 52bl NASA/Goddard/Arizona State University, 52-53b NASA/GSFC/Arizona State University, 53t NASA, 53cr NASA, 54t AstroStar, 54b Jair Ferreira Belafacce, 55b Thomas Dutour, 56t SP rabbito, 57t AZSTARMAN, 57bl Macrovector, 57br Alzinous/Creative Commons, 58bl Oldschool3d, 59t shooarts, 58-59b NASA/JPL, 59br NASA/Bill Ingalls, 60-61t Artsiom P, 60cl Federico Magonio, 60br Sebastian Sonnen, 61t NASA/JPL-Caltech, 61b Raymond Cassel, 62t Elenarts, 62b NASA, 63t David Hajnal, 63cr NASA/JPL, 63b delcarmat, 64-65t Nerthuz, 64-65c iztverichka, 64b NASA/JPL-Caltech/MSSS, 65cl, 65cr NASA/JPL-Caltech/University of Arizona, 66 Nerthuz, 67t NASA/JPL-Caltech/SwRI/MSSS/Gerald Eichstad/Sean Doran, 67cr NASA/JPL-Caltech/SwRI/MSSS, 67b AstroStar, 68t NASA/JPL-Caltech/SwRI/MSSS, 68bl MichaelTaylor, 68-69c Elena11, 69tl BreizhAtao, 69r ESA/AOES, 69b Elena11, 70c NASA/JPL/University of Colorado, 71t Dotted Yeti, 71bl NASA/JPL/

Space Science Institute, 71br Wellcome Trust, 72tl NASA/JPL/University of Colorado, 72-73c NASA / JPL-Caltech / Space Science Institute, 72b NASA/JPL-Caltech/Space Science Institute, 73tr Whitelion61, 73bl NASA, 74-75t, 74b buradaki, 75tr Jurik Peter, 76tl NASA/JPL-Caltech/UCLA/MPS/DLR/IDA, 76-77b NASA, 77t NASA/JPL-Caltech, 78tr, 78cr NASA, 78br NASA/JPL-Caltech/UCLA/MPS/DLR/IDA, 79t NASA/JPL, 79br NASA, 80tl NASA, 80br jorisvo, 81tl ESO/E. Slawik, 81tr NASA/SOFIA/Lynette Cook, 82tl Vadim Sadovski, 82b Nikta_Nikta, 83tr Matt Deakin, 83tc Pavel Chagochkin, 83b Makarov Konstantin, 84tr NASA, 84br USAF, 85 Dima Zel, 86-87, 87bl NASA, 87r Slatan, 88t sripfoto, 88cl Rlevente/Creative Commons, 89tr Anjo Kan, 89b NASA, 90bl Pyty, 90cr Ahmed92pk, 91l NASA/JPL-Caltech, 91br Jurik Peter, 92t ESA/Hubble & NASA, 92cl ESA/Hubble & NASA, G. Folatelli, 93tr Ahmed92pk, 93cr New York World-Telegram and the Sun Newspaper/Library of Congress, 96t Triff, 96b Morphart Creation, 98 Olha Polishchuk, 101b Vytautas Kielaitis, 103b Jurik Peter, 106t Piotr Velixar, 106b Yurumi, 107c NASA/JPL/University of Arizona, 111t Tragoolchitr Jittasaiyapan, 113b Matsumoto, 116b Malachi Jacobs, 117t NASA/STScI Digitized Sky Survey/Noel Carboni, 118-119b Matsumoto, 120b Allexxandar, 123t Pike-28, 126b AZSTARMAN, 128 Antares_StarExplorer, 129cr Tragoolchitr Jittasaiyapan, 131t Serrgey75, 131b Procy, 132-133t, 132-133b peresanz, 133cr CNG Coins/Creative Commons, 134t Brian Donovan, 135t Ezequiel Etcheverry, 136cr Marusya Chaika, 137l Martin Capek, 137br sciencepics, 138tr Pike-28, 138-139t NASA/Catholic University of America, 138-139b NASA, ESA, and N. Da Rio (University of Virginia): Processing: Gladys Kober (NASA/Catholic University of America), 139tl-r: NASA, Douglas James Butner, NASA, NASA, 139br Monika Wisniewska, 140t NASA, 140b Antares_StarExplorer, 141r NASA, 142t NASA, ESA, HEIC, and The Hubble Heritage Team (STScI/AURA), 142b Pawel Radomski, 143 NASA, ESA, C.R. O'Dell (Vanderbilt University), and M. Meixner, P. McCullough, and G. Bacon (Space Telescope Science Institute), 144t NASA, 144b Outer Space, 145 NASA, 146-147t NASA/CXC/M. Weiss, 146bl Allexxandar, 146br NASA, 147cl NASA, ESA, and The Hubble Heritage Team (STScI/AURA), 147bl NASA, 147br IAU/M. Zamani, 148tl Antares_StarExplorer, 149t NASA, ESA, P. Oesch (Yale University), G. Brammer (STScI), P. van Dokkum (Yale University), and G. Illingworth (University of California, Santa Cruz), 149b NASA/ESA and The Hubble Heritage Team (STScI), 150t AURORA Tomasz Zywczak, 151t NASA, 151bl Naci Yavuz, 152t NASA, 152-153b SRStudio, 154 SMCurator/Creative Commons, 155 Do Mi Nic, 156 Garry Basnett, 157 Bill Florence, 159 Elenarts

Every effort has been made to acknowledge correctly and contact the source and/or copyright holder of each picture. Any unintentional errors or omissions will be corrected in future editions of this book.